Springer Studies in the History of Economic Thought

This series offers an outlet for research in the history of economic thought. It features scholarly studies on important theoretical developments and great economic thinkers that have contributed to the evolution of the economic discipline.

Springer Studies in the History of Economic Thought (SSHET) welcomes proposals for research monographs, edited volumes and handbooks from a variety of disciplines that seek to study the history of economic thinking and help to arrive at a better understanding of modern economics. Relevant topics include, but are not limited to, various schools of thought, important pioneers and thinkers, ancient and medieval economic thought, mercantilism, cameralism and physiocracy, classical and neoclassical economics, historical, institutional and evolutionary economics, socialism and Marxism, Keynesian, Sraffian and Austrian economics, econometrics and mathematical studies as well as economic methodology and the link between economic history and history of economic thought.

All titles in this series are peer-reviewed.

For further information on the series and to submit a proposal for consideration, please contact Johannes Glaeser (Senior Editor Economics) Johannes.glaeser@springer.com.

Yasuo Gonjo · Kazuhiko Yago · Patrick Fridenson

The Truth of Liberal Economy

Jacques Rueff and John Maynard Keynes

Springer

Yasuo Gonjo (Deceased)
Yokohama National University
Yokohama, Japan

Patrick Fridenson
Centre de Recherches Historiques
Ecole des Hautes Etudes en Sciences Sociales
Paris, France

Kazuhiko Yago
School of Commerce
Waseda University
Shinjuku-ku, Japan

ISSN 2662-6098 ISSN 2662-6101 (electronic)
Springer Studies in the History of Economic Thought
ISBN 978-981-99-0840-0 ISBN 978-981-99-0841-7 (eBook)
https://doi.org/10.1007/978-981-99-0841-7

This Springer imprint is published by the registered company Springer Nature Singapore Pte Ltd.
The registered company address is: 152 Beach Road, #21-01/04 Gateway East, Singapore 189721, Singapore

Contents

Authors and Translator

About the Author

Yasuo Gonjo (1941–2021), emeritus professor, Yokohama National University. Outstanding economic historian, specialized in contemporary financial history of France. The field of research covers colonial banking, Banque de France, and European monetary integration. Long time interest in neoliberalism in Europe, to present a thoroughly alternative view of contemporary history of capitalism. Main publications include *French Imperialism and Asia: Bank of Indochina* (University of Tokyo Press, 1985), *Banque coloniale ou banque d'affaires: la Banque de l'Indochine sous la IIIe République* (Comité de l'histoire économique et financière de la France, 1993), *French Capitalism and the Central Bank: Modernization of Banque pour France* (University of Tokyo Press, 1999), *Historical Origin of Monetary Union: Transformation of the Capitalist World and the European Choice* (Nihon Keizai Hyouronsha, 2013). Nikkei Economic Literature Prize Laureate (1999), Order of the Sacred Treasure (2019).

About the Translator

Kazuhiko Yago (1962), professor, Waseda University. Economic historian specialized in international financial history. Mainly studying the international financial organizations (BIS, IMF and OECD) from historical perspectives. Main publications include *Public Finances and Popular Savings in France: Caisse des Dépôts et Consignations (1816–1944)* (University of Tokyo Press, 1999), *The Financial History of the Bank for International Settlements* (Routledge, 2013), *History of the IMF, Organization, Policy, and Market* (co-edited with Yoshio Asai and Masanao Itoh, Springer, 2015), *Handbook of the History of Money and Currency* (co-edited with Stefano Battilossi and Youssef Cassis, Springer, 2020). Representative Board (president) of Political Economy and Economic History Society, Japan (2019-2021). Prix Shibusawa Claudel Laureate (2000).

About the Author of the Postface and the Supplement to the Bibliography

Patrick Fridenson professor emeritus of International Business History at the Ecole des Hautes Etudes en Sciences Sociales (EHESS), Paris, France. His research deals with the strategies, innovations, ethics, structures, and performances of business enterprises in relation to consumers and to the regulatory and social environment in international perspective (comparisons between France, Germany, the United States, and Japan). He has worked on several industries: coal, automobile, aircraft, electronics. He is the author, co-author, or editor of several books, including *New Perspectives on 20th Century European Retailing* (London, 2021), *Ethical Capitalism. Shibusawa Eiichi and Business Leadership in Global Perspective* (Toronto, University of Toronto Press, 2017), *Reimagining Business History* (Baltimore, Johns Hopkins, 2013—translated in Japanese, 2017), *The Automobile Revolution* (Chapel Hill, NC, University of North Carolina Press, 1982, also available on Internet), *The French Home Front, 1914–1918* (Oxford, 1992), *Thomson's First Century* (Jouy-en-Josas, 1995), *Histoire des usines Renault*, vol. I (2nd ed., Paris, 1998), and the author of many articles. Beyond French, his articles have appeared in English, German, Spanish, and Japanese books or journals. He has been President of the French Association of Economic History (AFHE) and, in the United States, of the Business History Conference. He is a board member of the Comité d'histoire économique et financière (CHEFF) instituted by the French Ministry of Economy and Finance.

Chapter 1
Introduction: A Portrait of Jacques Rueff

Before mentioning the all-too-familiar economist, John Maynard Keynes, let me introduce the somewhat lesser known character of Jacques Rueff with a brief outline of his life, much of which is drawn from his autobiography (Rueff, 1977, vol. 1).

Jacques Léon Rueff was born in Paris on August 23, 1896, into a family of Jewish doctors. In April 1915, when Rueff was 18, and still in his first year at the prestigious Lycée Charlemagne, he was mobilized to serve in World War I which had begun the previous year. After his education and training as a cadet at Fontainebleau, he was sent to the front in January 1916 as an assistant lieutenant (later promoted to lieutenant) and to be moved from place to place among the bloody battlefields of Somme and Verdun. In July 1918, due to his English-speaking ability, Rueff was assigned to the U.S. Army as a liaison officer, and thereafter accompanied the U.S. Army in counter-offensives against Germany on the northern and eastern fronts. Rueff was awarded the Medal of Honor for his military service three times during the war.

In the summer of 1919, soon after the peace treaty was signed in Versailles, the Ecole Polytechnique, a famous institution for training technocrats, held an entrance examination for students who had gone to war. Rueff passed the exam and entered the Ecole in the fall of the same year. There, he met Clément Colson, a professor of economics, through whom he learned about the neoclassical economics of Walras, Jevons, Marshall, and others. Two years later, he graduated from the Ecole Polytechnique and became a professor at the Institute of Statistics of the University of Paris. (He later became a professor at the *Institut d'Etudes Politiques de Paris.*) In September 1923, he was hired as a financial inspector (*inspecteur des finances*) at the French Ministry of Economy and Finance (hereinafter abbreviated as the Ministry of Finance), a position known as a gateway to the highest ranks of the financial bureaucracy. According to Rueff, two things contributed to his choice of finance as a profession while simultaneously working as a professor of economics. The first was that he had written a philosophical book, "From Physical to Moral Sciences" (*Des sciences physiques aux sciences morales*) (Rueff, 1922), which he had been working

Y. Gonjo et al., *The Truth of Liberal Economy*, Springer Studies in the History of Economic Thought, https://doi.org/10.1007/978-981-99-0841-7_1

on while he was a student at the Ecole Polytechnique, and had developed his own scientific methodology. The other was that he had studied economics at the Ecole.

Rueff, like Keynes, chose to be a financial bureaucrat; however, unlike Keynes, he also worked as a university professor throughout his entire career as a financial bureaucrat. During his career, he was seconded to the League of Nations Secretariat in Geneva from 1927 to 1930, and then to the French Embassy in London from 1930 to 1934, all the while returning to Paris once a week and never missing a lecture at the university.

During his time in Geneva, he visited Eastern European countries as an envoy of the Financial Committee of the League of Nations. In 1930, while in London, he visited Japan and China (Tianjin and Beijing) via New York. His visit to Japan was at the invitation of the Japanese government, and he gave a report on the unemployment problem at a research meeting of the International Statistical Institute in Tokyo, and also gave a lecture at the Industrial Club of Japan on the stabilization of the franc, which he was involved with under Prime Minister Raymond Poincaré. The lecture at the Industrial Club of Japan was moderated by Junnosuke Inoue, the Minister of Finance who had just lifted the gold ban. When Inoue introduced Rueff to the audience, he is reported to have said, "I have only implemented the policies of Mr. Poincaré" (Rueff, 1977, vol. 1, p. 71). The following year, in October 1931, he joined the delegation led by Prime Minister Pierre Laval to the United States in his capacity as Deputy Finance Minister and was present at the meeting between Laval and President Herbert Hoover. The ambitious and energetic activities of the young Rueff can clearly be seen.

Rueff returned from London at the end of 1934 and was appointed assistant director of the General Fund Department (*Direction du Mouvement Général des Fonds*, later renamed the Treasury Department, i.e., *Direction du Trésor* during the war). He was promoted to Deputy Director (in charge of international finance) in April 1935, and then to Director General in November 1936 during the Popular Front regime. The General Fund Department was the most powerful government department in France, with the powers of the International Bureau and the Financial Bureau of the Ministry of Finance. Rueff remained in his position even after the Popular Front entered a phase of collapse in 1938. In September 1939, on the eve of the outbreak of war with Germany, he resigned from the Ministry of Finance and became Deputy Governor of the Bank of France. However, when France was defeated in the early stages of the war against Germany, and a government of collaboration with Germany was established in Vichy in central France, Rueff was forced to resign his position as Deputy Governor (in January 1941) because of his Jewish background, and he retreated to a remote village in the department of Ardèche. With the end of World War II, he returned to public life as head of the International Reparations Institute. Later, when three Communities were founded by six continental European countries, he became a judge of their Courts of Justice. For 10 years, he was the only judge with a background in economics to be involved in the operation of the Common Market. Since he had been advocating the establishment of a Common Market in the European region since 1929, his appointment as a judge of the Court of Justice was not surprising.

Rueff's representative achievements as an economic and financial expert are as follows: Calculation of the new parity for the stabilization of the franc in 1928 (de facto stabilization in 1926); writing a draft of the European Union for Foreign Minister Aristide Briand (1929); formulation of monetary doctrine in France during the Great Depression (1930–33); managing the turbulent and difficult economic and fiscal management under the People's Front regime (1936–39); reform of France's fiscal and economic structure under Charles de Gaulle's administration, and lastly, proposals for reform of the international monetary system (1958–60).

As a researcher, Rueff was both a philosopher and one of France's leading economists. Although a financial bureaucrat, he frequently lectured as an economic theorist and authored numerous works (monographs, articles, pamphlets, and newspaper editorials). His first monograph was the aforementioned philosophical book, "From Physical to Moral Sciences," (*Des Sciences physiques aux sciences morales*) published by Alcan in Paris in 1922 (Rueff, 1922), the year he graduated from the Ecole Polytechnique. This book was translated into English in 1954 by Oxford University Press and Johns Hopkins University Press and was a great success in the English-speaking world. Two American jurists wrote forewords to the English translation, and economist Simon Kuznets read the text and advised the translators.

Rueff's inspiration for "From Physical to Moral Sciences" came when he was an 18-year-old student at the Lycée and was triggered by his discovery of the existence of non-Euclidean geometry. Some scholars have tried to relate this first work to the logical positivism or new positivism of Ernst Mach, Henri Poincaré, and Ludwig Wittgenstein (Bourricaud et Salin, 1989, pp. 93–99; Chivvis, 2010, p. 21). However, Rueff himself did not refer to these currents in positivist philosophy.

It was his mentor, Colson, who encouraged Rueff to publish the manuscript as a single work. Before publication, however, he visited Henri Bergson at his private residence, wearing his lieutenant's uniform, the uniform of the Ecole Polytechnique, to seek the opinion of this great scholar. After reading the manuscript, Bergson said, "Ripe fruit must be dropped from the tree," and recommended its publication (Rueff, 1977, vol. 1, p. 29).

Rueff's representative works in the field of economics are "The Theory of Monetary Phenomena" (Rueff, 1927) and "Social Order" (Rueff, 1945). The latter, a book of basic theories that straddle monetary theory and sociology, is a massive two-volume work with a total of 747 pages and was Rueff's life's work. By 1981, it had been reprinted four times. It was also translated and published in German, Spanish, and Italian, with Wilhelm Röpke writing the preface to the German translation. Between 1977, the last year of Rueff's activity, and 1981, the year of his death, the six-volume "Rueff's Complete Works" (Rueff, 1977–81) was published in Paris. It was planned by the New York-based Lehrman Institute to be published in English as well as in French. In fact, the cover of the French edition is labeled as if an English edition existed. However, there is no evidence that the English version ever appeared on the market.

Rueff was nominated as a member of the French Academy in 1965. In 1967, a collection of articles entitled "Philosophical Foundations of the Economic

System" (Rueff, 1967) was published to commemorate his 60th birthday. Twenty-six economists and philosophers, mostly leading members of the Mont Pèlerin Society, an international organization of neoliberals, contributed to this collection, including, for example, Wilhelm Röpke, Friedrich von Hayek, Ludwig Erhard, Milton Friedman, Robert V. Roosa, Oskar Morgenstern, Karl Popper, and Maurice Allais. It should be noted that among them are some of the biggest names in German politics, as well as former officials of the U.S. Treasury.

Since the nineteenth century, it has not been uncommon for French bureaucrats to be active in the field of economics, but it has been rare for a man in Rueff's position to have made first-rate achievements in various fields. In 1996, on the 100th anniversary of his birth, the French government held a series of commemorative events to honor his achievements, including a symposium, the issuance of commemorative stamps and coins bearing his portrait, and the construction of a small square in his name. Three speakers at the symposium were James Tobin and Maurice Allais, Nobel laureates in economics who knew Rueff personally, and Robert A. Mandel, who would receive the prize a few years later.

As shown above, Rueff's career and accomplishments were remarkable. As a theorist, he was feared by the financial bureaucracy for his "Newtonian" abilities. In the 1960s, he became a man of the time as a harsh critic of Keynesian theory and the post-World War II international monetary system (i.e., the Bretton Woods system), and his work was widely covered by the Western media. In France, however, he was often marginalized. Protectionism and statecraft have been deeply rooted in the country since the days of Colbert in the late seventeenth century, and this tradition could not be easily broken, not even by Rueff.

From the mid-1980s, after Rueff's death, the neoliberal structural reforms that he had initiated began to be implemented systematically in France. Along with this, a movement to reevaluate Rueff appeared. The aforementioned commemorative event in 1996 is a typical example, but there were also two other large-scale symposiums. One was held by the de Gaulle Institute in January 1985, in which economists, former prime ministers and economic ministers, and former economic and financial bureaucrats, participated as presenters and discussants (Institut Charles de Gaulle, 1986). The second was a symposium of economists organized by IPAG (Paris Graduate School of Business) in May 2001. Rueff's economic and social theories and his numerous policy proposals have survived the times as classics, at least in integrated Europe and especially in the French-speaking world, and as unparalleled examples of attempts to put the economy and society on the right track.

Part I
New Economic, Social and Political Issues and Economic Theory: Introductory Note

About Adjustment: An Explanation The term "adjustment" (adjustment in English, *ajustement* in French) appears as a leitmotif throughout this book. The meaning of the term varies slightly depending on the context in which it is used, and the way it is used in economics is somewhat confusing. So let us briefly explain the meaning of the term "adjustment" in the context of Rueff's work.

Take wheat production as an example. Let's say that wheat production declines due to crop failure. The supply of wheat to the market will decrease and the price of wheat will increase. Part of the demand will not like the high price of wheat and will turn to wheat substitutes. The price of the substitute will rise, and in response, the substitute will be produced more, increasing its supply to the market. Thus, the price of wheat settles down. In other words, the market has found a new equilibrium point and equilibrium is restored. As we can see from this example, when there is a change in one part of the production activity, this change affects the production and supply of other commodities in the market through changes in prices. As a result, the effects of the causal event (the increase in the price of wheat) is canceled out, hence, the shock to the market is relatively short-lived. This phenomenon is called adjustment, and its basis is the feedback mechanism widely known in the field of cybernetics.

The role of prices in the fluctuations of wheat production is played by the rate of interest in the realm of credit, and by the international movement of gold and exchange rates, in addition to prices in the realm of international economic transactions. Since credit usually intervenes in wheat production, and its fluctuations affect foreign trade, the actual adjustment is quite complicated.

The above explanation assumes that the degree of crop failure is within a certain range. The situation would be different if a severe crop failure persisted for many years. This is because more and more farmers will withdraw from wheat production and a large number of agricultural workers will become unemployed. The emergence of unemployed people looking for work puts pressure on the labor market. Wage levels will fall, pushing down the living standards of all workers. The problem becomes more than just an adjustment; it becomes a social and even a political problem. Thus, in a free market economy, a crisis in one sector of the economy can trigger a social or political crisis through the price mechanism.

The adjustments that come with a free market economy sometimes cause unbearable pain to the members of society. This raises several issues and questions. Can we let the market do all the work? Shouldn't public authorities intervene and control the market? Is there such a thing as adjustment or is it a fiction? Isn't the problem that is supposed to be caused by the market economy actually caused by the dysfunction of the price mechanism due to the intervention of public authorities? These were the sort of problems and questions that were behind the Rueff/Keynes controversy. The same issues were deeply involved in Rueff's dealings with the economic and financial officials of the West, including the U.S., on the issue of the dollar and the international monetary system after the death of Keynes, as well as the birth of a new concept of liberalism called neoliberalism in Paris in the late 1930s. The market economy may seem simple at first glance, but within it lie complex and subtle problems.

Chapter 2
The Economic Consequences of World War I: Keynes and Rueff

World War I, which began in July 1914, was the first great war in history, with 70 million adult males sent to battlefields throughout the belligerent countries. The fighting ended in November 1918 with the signing of an armistice between France and Germany. The Peace Conference was held in Paris in January 1919, and the Peace Treaty was signed between the Allies and Germany in Versailles in June of the same year. During the 4 years and 3 months of uninterrupted fighting, as many as 10 million soldiers lost their lives. Taking France as an example, where the main battles were fought, 1,500,000 people, or 10.5% of the country's male working population, were killed or missing in action. This greatly distorted the demographic composition of France for a long time. The social capital destroyed during the war which included houses, industrial facilities, roads, railroads, canals, and ports, was unprecedented in scale. Thus, in January 1921, the Allied Reparations Commission presented Germany with a staggering reparation claim of 132 billion gold marks.

The impact of the World War on European countries was enormous. After the end of the war, the political, social, and economic systems of these countries, as well as the ideologies and philosophies that had supported them, had to be fundamentally reexamined. It was at this turning point in history that Rueff and Keynes began to engage in the study of economics in earnest.

2.1 Keynes

Keynes attended the Paris Peace Conference as a representative of the British Treasury and was present at this historic meeting. Disappointed with the process of the conference and its outcome, he resigned from the Treasury and, at the end of 1920, published his famous book, "The Economic Consequences of Peace" (Keynes, 1919/1971).

In this work, Keynes analyzes the Great War from the perspective of an economist, placing economics within the context of history. What is particularly noteworthy

Y. Gonjo et al., *The Truth of Liberal Economy*, Springer Studies in the History of Economic Thought, https://doi.org/10.1007/978-981-99-0841-7_2

is his understanding of the changes in the situation before and after the war as follows: Since the 1870s, the economies of European countries were united through the market and the dynamic center shifted from the former Britain and France to the newly industrialized Germany. The postwar economic recovery began in Germany, which in turn led to the recovery of the British and French economies, followed by the recovery of the Eastern European economies. Therefore, claiming reparations that exceeded Germany's ability to pay would hinder Germany's recovery and delay the postwar recovery of other European countries. On the grounds of this analysis, Keynes harshly denounced French Prime Minister Georges Clemenceau, who led the conference, for his retributionist approach which was, in turn, followed by the leaders of Britain and the United States.

After this, Keynes, as is well known, broke away from the traditional economics of the nineteenth century and proceeded to write vigorously for the construction of new economics. Immediately after the Paris Peace Conference, he began to publish a series of essays with innovative content dealing with postwar economic issues in a variety of media, including monographs, magazines, and pamphlets.

In these works, he made famous statements such as "In the long run we will all be dead" (*A Tract on Monetary Reform*) (Keynes, 1923/1971, vol. IV) and insisted that the task for economists is to "redefine the distinction between what the government should and should not do" (*The End of Laissez-Faire*) (Keynes, 1926/1978, vol. IX). He demonstrated the drastic paradigm shifts in the fields of philosophy, politics, and economics ensuing after World War I, based on a bold and clear analysis of many examples. In the economic field, he strongly suggested the following points. Price stability should be the social goal rather than exchange rate stability, and it is more rational to choose inflation rather than deflation as an economic policy. Therefore, it is unrealistic to restore the gold standard. Improvements in the "operating techniques of modern capitalism," particularly the "prudent control of currency and credit by central institutions" (*The End of Laissez-Faire*), would be useful, and he saw the introduction of a managed currency system as an irreversible trend.

In this way, Keynes rejected the idea of reviving the gold standard (full gold standard) that had been adopted by major countries before World War I. Instead, he supported the adoption of a managed gold standard (managed currency system), arguing for the usefulness of wisdom-based monetary and credit management of the market economy. All his arguments caused a stir among policymakers and intellectuals in Western countries.

2.2 Rueff's Philosophy and His Studies on Exchange

Unlike Keynes, Rueff did not directly comment on World War I. However, his first book, "From Physical to Moral Sciences," (Rueff, 1922) and his article "Exchange, a Natural Phenomenon," both published in 1922, show that his view of the Great War was contrary to Keynes's and show why he regarded Keynes as his opponent throughout his life. Though not very comprehensive owing to being limited to the period of the early 1920s, we can clearly see in these two works what can be called the prototype of Rueff's thought and theory (much as Keynes's *The Economic Consequences of Peace* and *A Tract on Monetary Reform* reflected his). Therefore, I will introduce the central points of these two works to the extent that they are relevant to the subject of this book.

"From Physical to Moral Sciences" (Original Version in 1922)

This work deals with the question of the "character of scientific explanation." Rueff examines, with many examples, how scientific explanations are made, referring to individual sciences, from material sciences such as geometry, theoretical mechanics and celestial mechanics, physics and chemistry, biology, etc., to human sciences such as psychology, moral science, and economics. Rueff examines the nature of how scientific explanations are made with many supporting examples.

The human mind's perception of the external world is based on the discovery of a series of ongoing relationships between things. These relations are called "laws." The "theory" of science, or "science" as it is called, attempts to show these empirically ascertainable relations as necessarily arising from the "nature of things," that is, as logically inevitable. However, "scientific explanation is not based on causes that exist in nature as objective entities, independent of the method of observation. It is a set of proposed axioms, canons, and definitions created and chosen by scholars. In other words, "scientific theories are nothing more than a system of premises that make it possible to replace the observable causal connections in nature with the [logical] causal connections that our mind needs" (Rueff, 1979, vol. II–1, p. 30). Thus, Rueff concludes that scientific explanation, or the construction of science, is "the creation of causes."

Rueff then goes on to claim that the above is common to all sciences, regardless of whether they are material or human sciences. He devotes the largest number of pages to political economy (hereinafter referred to as "economics") to which he has devoted his life, and which he regards as no exception to the above. In economics, too, events obtained by observation of the external world are collected and formulated as laws expressing the common character of any given group of events, that is, laws concerning the prices of goods and services and the fluctuations of those prices. These laws are nothing more than the relationships between the day-to-day, moment-to-moment actions of countless people, just like the relationships between particles of gas in suspension. However, by establishing axioms and definitions, we construct logical laws, or theories, from these relationships, such as the law of supply and demand, the theory of monopoly prices, and so on. In this way, a theory is created to recognize the existence of the true nature of things through a rather strict method of deduction.

The fact that there are laws in the economy does not mean that people are slaves to the laws. By knowing the laws of economics, one can devise a technology called "policy" and use this technology to achieve the goals that one has set for oneself. It is similar to how a person can fly an airplane despite the presence of gravity. In other words, the relationship between mathematical economics and policy technology is the same as the relationship between physics and aeronautics. Incidentally, in this book, Rueff repeatedly stresses the usefulness of using mathematics in economics. Not content to stop there, he borrows a definition from Leon Walras and develops his economic theory in mathematical form over 23 pages.

Rueff suggests that theories in science are purely intellectual discoveries of various causes and do not reflect the truth itself, so they can be "right" or "wrong" in light of the true nature of things. In the case of physics, advances in observation and experimental methods can negate theories that were previously considered correct. In the realm of economics and society, an imbalance in political dynamics and a shift in the system may result in the failure of previous theories. Rueff explains this using the terms "Euclidean" and "non-Euclidean," popularized by the mathematician Henri Poincaré. When theories and institutions are consistent with reality, they are Euclidean; when they are at odds with reality, they are non-Euclidean. In addition, the same theory or system can be Euclidean or non-Euclidean depending on the conditions under which it is applied. In the introduction to the second edition of this work, Rueff later explained, using Keynes as an example, that Keynesian theory implicitly assumes the wage invariance hypothesis that wages are unaffected by the market. Under such conditions, it is true that only Keynesian thinking is valid, so his theory can be said to be Euclidean. In the West, however, the wage invariance hypothesis is not valid because wages (especially their increase) are still determined by changes in aggregate demand. Hence, in this context, Keynesian theory is non-Euclidean (Rueff, 1979, vol. II–1, p. 39).

In his book "From Physical to Moral Sciences," Rueff develops two principles of method that would later guide his economic research. One is a principle related to society and the other is to thought and ideology.

> We now know that it makes no sense to justify the reality of society by rational theories. Moral and economic theories cannot determine the form of our society any more than kinetics can create the characteristics of a gas. Society is realized and exists by the whole workings of the universe. Also, the theories we have are currently Euclidean, but will probably not be so in the future. These theories are merely created by induction to reproduce the laws (Rueff, 1979, vol. II-1, p. 145).

This quote shows that Rueff had arrived at a kind of materialism and relativism. As will become clear in Part II, his discourse on current economic issues was always principled. His criticism of Keynes and Milton Friedman was very harsh, and his economics has been criticized for its inflexibility. This perceived inflexibility in his discourse may be considered a result of his conviction expressed in the above quote that: "Moral and economic theories cannot determine the form of our society any more than kinetics can create the characteristics of gas."

The second principle central to the book is his emphasis on empirical research.

> A fundamental part of all the moral sciences will be the exploration of empirical laws. The materials available to facilitate this search are history, statistics, and market price lists of all kinds. Only by studying them systematically will it be possible to discover new laws and to verify rational laws that are assumed to be true (Rueff, 1979, vol. II-1, p. 146).

Rueff's emphasis on the empirical in his economic research and his interest in the relationship between theory and reality, already evident here, will continue to be hallmarks of his work.

"Exchange, a Natural Phenomenon" (1922)

This paper was recommended by the mathematician Emile Borel and was published in the General Sciences Journal of the French Academy. It was unusual for a renowned mathematician to recommend a paper on economics to a prestigious scientific journal, moreover, the maiden paper of a young researcher who had studied economics for only 2 years at university. According to Rueff, this was because of the use of econometrics, a novel method at the time. The paper was published and received a great response. It was groundbreaking for approaching the "phenomenon" of exchange rates from both theoretical and empirical perspectives, as well as for its methodology.

In this paper, Rueff formulates his theory of exchange based on the following two principles. Principle 1: The purchasing power of each country's currency does not deviate significantly from that of the other countries as long as the currencies are issued on the basis of commercial transactions. Principle 2: The "divergence" between the domestic purchasing power of country 1's currency and the purchasing power of country 2's currency (expressed in country 1's currency) serves to adjust the balance of payments and maintain equilibrium (or restore the balance of payments equilibrium that has been temporarily disturbed). The "deviation" (*disparité*) here is defined by the following formula.[1]

$$\pi_{1\cdot 1} - \frac{1}{C_{1\cdot 2}}\pi_{2\cdot 2} = P_{1\cdot 2}$$

The inward purchasing power of a currency is defined by the following formula, where A is the inward purchasing power of the currency of country 2 in country 1, B is the inward purchasing power of the currency of country 2 in country 1, and C is the inward purchasing power of the currency of country 2 in country 1. The inward purchasing power of a currency is defined by the following formula, where 100 is divided by the wholesale price index at the time.

$$\frac{100}{I}$$

Rueff first proves that the two principles are true theoretically using the econometric method. In other words, he proves that the two principles are true without setting any new conditions.

He then uses statistical data to prove that the two principles are in fact true. He uses data from seven countries, including France, Britain, the United States, Italy, Belgium, Spain, and Switzerland, for the years 1912–13 and 1920–22. However, the official statistics on the balance of payments of all the countries were extremely poor, and virtually the only thing that could be tracked reliably during these periods was trade. Rueff carefully weighs the impact of these incomplete statistics on his

[1] The article "Exchange, a Natural Phenomenon" is revised and enlarged, to be contained in *Théorie des phénomènes monétaires* (Rueff, 1927). In the latter edition, the "deviation" is conveniently induced directly from the exchange rates, instead of the purchasing power parity. See Rueff (1979, vol. II-1, p. 305 et passim).

conclusions and judges the impact to be minimal. He then proceeds with the following steps in his testimony.

(1) The monthly purchasing power parity of the franc during the gold standard period of 1901–10 is calculated from the wholesale price index, and this average value is adopted as the reference unit for purchasing power.
(2) Calculate the monthly changes in the purchasing power (in francs) of the franc in seven countries, including France, for the 3-year period 1920–22. The results of this calculation confirm that the "divergence" in the purchasing power of the franc was very slight in all countries. We conclude that Principle 1 has been proven correct.
(3) For the same 3 years, 1920–22, calculate the monthly deviation between the purchasing power of the franc in France and the purchasing power of the franc in the other six countries. Then, we will show the results and the monthly balance of trade (special trade) in graphs and confirm that the fluctuations of the two correspond perfectly with a certain time difference. We conclude that the correctness of Principle 2 as well as that of Principle 1 has been demonstrated.

The graph shown below (see Fig. 2.1) is one of the seven graphs prepared by Rueff and is a summary chart. It shows the average "deviation" of the purchasing power of the franc in the seven countries and the monthly variation of the balance of trade (special trade) of France, respectively. From this figure, we can see that the fluctuations of the two curves correspond roughly with each other with a time lag of up to 2 months if we look at the corresponding maximum and minimum points.

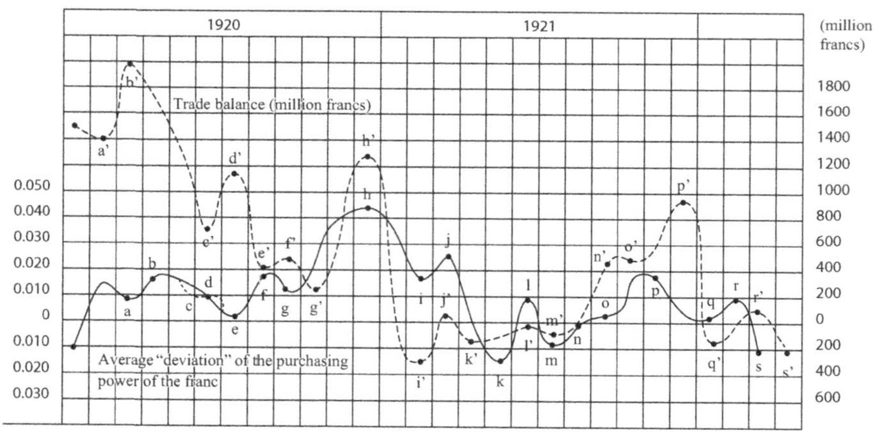

Fig. 2.1 Average deviation of the purchasing power of the franc in foreign countries and the balance of trade (special trade) of France (1920–1922). *Note* (1) "Foreign countries" refer to United Kingdom, United States, and Italy for 1920, United Kingdom, United States, Italy, Belgium, Spain, and Switzerland for 1921–1922. *Note* (2) "deviation" means monthly average deviation between the purchasing power of the franc in France and in the foreign countries. *Source* (Rueff, 1979, vol. II-2, p. 164)

Rueff concludes in summary that: the mechanism of automatic recovery of the balance of payments has been functioning consistently not only before the Great War under the gold standard but also after the war when the gold standard was suspended. In the postwar period, however, equilibrium is achieved through exchange rate fluctuations, a kind of price mechanism. This phenomenon in the balance of payments is no different from the restoration of equilibrium through the shifting of equilibrium points, which is widely known in the fields of physics and chemistry, such as Van't Hoff's law and Le Chatelier's law. It was precisely for this reason that Rueff chose "Exchange, a Natural Phenomenon" as the title of his paper.

In the last part of his paper, Rueff discusses in detail the policy implications of the phenomenon of balance of payments adjustment in relation to the German reparations problem. The content of the paper is still rough but it overlaps with a later paper dealing with the transfer problem. The conclusion of this paper was as follows. As long as neighboring countries do not restrict imports from Germany, and as long as the functioning of the price mechanism in Germany is not impaired, the transfer of reparations from Germany to the paying partner country is possible.

In both works described above, "From Physical to Moral Sciences" and "Exchange, a Natural Phenomenon," Rueff made two important propositions that fundamentally distinguish him from Keynes. First, as long as freedom is guaranteed to the individual, economic laws will continue to operate as strictly as the laws of physics. Therefore, economic policies must be formulated on the basis of economic laws, or microeconomic theory, as it is called in today's economics. Second, even though the economic environment in Europe changed drastically after the World War I, the balance of payments has nonetheless been restored to equilibrium by changes in the "divergence" of purchasing power of currencies among countries. Therefore, adjustment through the price mechanism is strictly in place and capable of overcoming various obstacles.

Thus, the classical theory of economics is still true both theoretically and empirically, that is, the classical theory of equilibrium is still Euclidean. Rueff derived the first proposition from his speculations on scientific explanations and the second proposition from his theoretical and empirical studies of the economy. This means that, in contrast to Keynes, Rueff came to recognize the continuity of economic society from before to after World War I. Rueff later called the phenomenon he identified in his article "Exchange, a Natural Phenomenon" the "phenomenon of monetary adjustment" and made it the cornerstone of his economics.

Chapter 3
"Permanent Unemployment" and the Unemployment Insurance System in the United Kingdom

During World War I, unanimous cabinets were formed in Britain and France, and leaders of left-wing parties and people from trade unions participated in the exercise of political power. As a result, when peace returned, the trade union movement gained momentum and left-wing parties increased their seats in the National Assembly. In Britain, a Labour Party government came to power in 1922, and in France, a left-wing coalition government was formed in 1924. In France, the Communist Party, which was part of the international communist movement, won 24 seats in the national election of 1924. Similar movements to these were seen in other European countries and the trend was also evident in the international organizations that emerged after the Great War. At the end of 1919, the International Labor Organization (ILO) was established as a sister organization of the League of Nations, and Albert Thomas, a French socialist, was appointed as the first Director General. One of its important tasks was to study the causes of unemployment and unemployment insurance systems and to collect unemployment statistics (Bureau international du travail, 1931, pp. 217–226). Clearly, the issue of unemployment had become a major concern both socially and politically.

In December 1925, Rueff published an article entitled "The Changes of Unemployment in Britain" in the French journal *Revue politique et parlementaire* (Rueff, 1925/1979, vol. II-2, pp. 219–230). This was the first study in the world to focus on a new type of unemployment—"permanent unemployment" as Rueff put it, as opposed to natural or cyclical unemployment. He wrote another paper on the same subject in the spring of 1931. The approach he adopted in both papers was diametrically opposed to the approach Keynes was to undertake in *The General Theory of Employment, Interest, and Money*.

Y. Gonjo et al., *The Truth of Liberal Economy*, Springer Studies in the History of Economic Thought, https://doi.org/10.1007/978-981-99-0841-7_3

3.1 Changes in Unemployment in the United Kingdom

In Britain, the number of unemployed began to increase rapidly in 1922, and since then the number has grown to well over 2,500,000. Rueff took up the issue of unemployment in Britain not only because the number of unemployed in this country was unusually high. Employment statistics are indispensable for the study of unemployment problems, and at that time, Britain was the only country where these statistics existed on a country basis.

Rueff's 1925 paper was relatively short, and his argument was simple. He constructed four curves from economic and employment statistics for the United Kingdom (see Fig. 3.1) and identified the following points. The two curves in the lower part of the figure are created and the following points are confirmed. Curves (a) and (b) in the lower part of the figure show (wholesale) price and wage indices, which rise simultaneously until mid-1920. Then, the price index (a) plummets and stays at the level of 150 after 1922. On the other hand, the wage index (b) continued to rise until the beginning of 1921, then gradually declined and began to rise again from the beginning of 1924. In contrast, the two curves in the upper panel, the unemployment rate and the real wage index, which are obtained by dividing the wage index by the price index, consistently move in tandem with each other.

Next, Rueff proceeds with his argument as follows. The reason why the unemployment rate in Britain has remained high is that wages have not fallen in line with prices, especially since the end of 1921. Rueff offers two reasons why wages have not fallen. The first is the "traditional" power of labor unions. At the end of 1921, the British National Currency, the pound sterling, returned to the gold standard at a higher-than-actual prewar parity. This caused the pound to be overvalued and domestic industry to suffer a recession. In a recession, wages are supposed to fall. However, the strength of the labor unions prevented wages from being lowered. The second reason is the British "unemployment relief policy," or the unemployment insurance system introduced in 1911. This system functions as a guarantee of a minimum wage because when wages fall below a certain level, workers choose to become unemployed and try to obtain unemployment insurance. Hence, according to Rueff, the "root cause" of the persistence of unemployment in the United Kingdom is the unemployment insurance system.

Because of these particular circumstances, if the unemployment rate was to fall in the United Kingdom, either prices would rise while wages would remain unchanged, or wages would be lowered without prices falling. However, neither of these is possible without causing a revolution or riot. Therefore, Rueff concludes, the unemployment rate in Britain will never return to the low level it was before the Great War.

Rueff's article was introduced by the economist and banker Josiah Stamp in the Financial Times on March 15, 1926, and became widely known in Europe, not only in French-speaking countries, and not only among economists. At the ILO in Geneva, the Director General, Albert Thomas, took great interest in Rueff's paper, saying

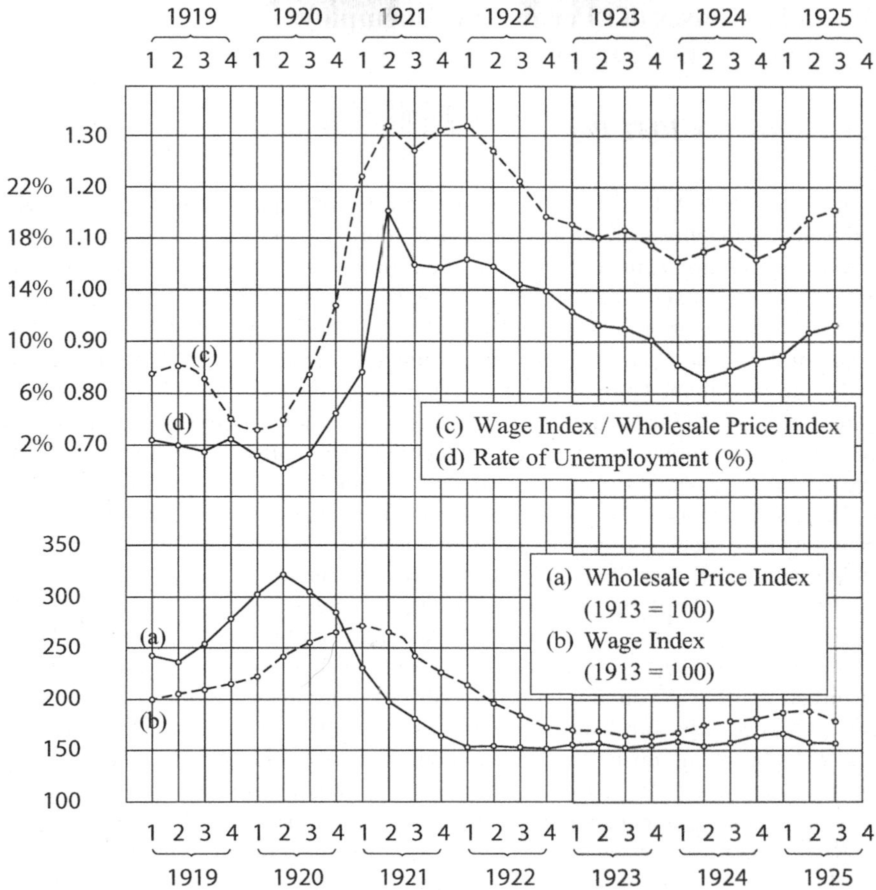

Fig. 3.1 Variation of unemployment in the United Kingdom (1919–25). *Source* (Rueff, 1979, vol. II-2, p. 226)

that it was important for workers to understand the causes of unemployment (Rueff, 1977, vol. I, pp. 87–88).

3.2 The Causes of "Permanent Unemployment" and Keynes's Response

3.2.1 *Rueff's 1931 Paper*

In March–April 1931, more than 5 years after his 1925 paper, Rueff anonymously published a lengthy article, in the French Journal of Political Economy, *Revue d'économie politique*, titled "Unemployment Insurance System—Causes of Permanent Unemployment" (Rueff,1931/1979, vol. II-2, pp. 219–230). It was accompanied by a short introduction by Charles Rist, editor-in-chief of the journal and a leading figure of the French Economic Society, stating that the author was a researcher who was familiar with the United Kingdom. At the time, the Great Depression was gripping European countries in earnest, and skepticism about the free market economy was spreading among various social categories. The author's name was withheld because his position at the time was that of a financial officer stationed in London, and diplomatic considerations were necessary. Nevertheless, it was clear to everyone who the anonymous author was, since the introduction to the article stated that the author had also written "Unemployment in Britain" in 1925.

In his paper, Rueff extends the period under study to 1931 and applies the same empirical analysis as in the 1925 paper. According to his analysis, the correlation between the two curves of the real wage index and the unemployment rate was disturbed in 1926–27 due to the general strike. Other than that, the two curves are perfectly positively correlated as they were before 1925. Therefore, unless there is a major change in circumstances, such as an increase in domestic prices due to protectionist trade policies, or a significant increase in productivity due to technological progress, unemployment should not decrease in the future.

Rueff's aim was not only to reconfirm the correctness of the 1925 article; he had another motive. Although several eminent economists, such as Josiah Stamp, William Beveridge, and Charles Rist, had given positive evaluations of Rueff's analysis and conclusions, many other experts and ordinary people remained silent and refused to clarify their positions. Rueff's main purpose of writing this paper was to ask why this is so and to criticize this attitude.

3.2.2 *Rueff's Claims Do not Fit with the Current Trends*

According to Rueff, the most significant point of the 1925 paper is that it proves through statistical analysis that there is a strong positive correlation between changes in real wages (wage index/general price index) and changes in the unemployment rate. Some of his critics admit the existence of this correlation. However, they believe that the rise in real wages is only one cause among many, and that unemployment has not decreased in the United Kingdom mainly because of changes in the market and industrial structures which became more pronounced after the war. This attitude is reflected, for example, in the lengthy research report prepared by the ILO's Unemployment Commission in 1931. The report concludes with the following words.

> Thus, the case studies conducted at different times and for different countries clearly show that there is a correlation between *changes in the price level and changes in unemployment*. It is also clear that measures must be taken to prevent *a severe recession and a period of low prices* from occurring in the future. (Author's italics) (Bureau international du travail, Commission du chômage, «les fluctuations monétaires et chômages», Studies and Reports of the International Labour Office, Series C, No.16, Geneva, 1931, cited in Rueff, 1979, vol. II-2, p. 246)

Alternatively, Rueff argued as follows: the ILO report is about classic cyclical unemployment, not the new type of unemployment. If British unemployment is cyclical unemployment, the unemployment rate should have fallen in 1925 when the general price index fell. However, there has been no change in the unemployment rate at all. The unemployment is thus "permanent." The problem with unemployment in Britain is not the change in the general price index, but the price of one commodity (wages) relative to other prices, i.e., the "relative price" (wages/general price index). Therefore, we should ask why the wage index has remained at a higher level than the general price index since the end of 1922.

Rueff continues as follows: the level of wages that has remained high is the level set by the collective agreement. Such a level can be maintained in the face of massive unemployment only because of the unemployment insurance system, which is in reality a state guarantee in name only. "'Unemployment benefits' act as an infinite guarantee of trade union discipline. This is the essential device that stabilizes wages at a level completely independent of the price index, and this is the cause of permanent unemployment" (Rueff, 1979, vol. II-2, pp. 244–245). According to Rueff, the problem goes beyond that. Since wages no longer fluctuate, the British labor market is no longer in equilibrium, and there is no longer a redistribution of labor, all of which create an extremely serious situation.

The above phenomenon is seen only in the United Kingdom and not in countries without unemployment insurance systems, except for Germany, where wages are set by force. So, according to Rueff, we should see the same phenomenon wherever the price mechanism is hindered.

Why are so many experts and lay people silent on Rueff's analysis and the claims so logically contained in this analysis? According to Rueff, there are two possible reasons. First, Rueff's argument is contrary to both the social conventions and the current postwar trend of "organizing the economy." Secondly, it is incompatible with the "idealism" prevailing among prominent people. In short, Rueff says that his argument does not fit the current of the times.

In the last chapter, Rueff sums up the entire paper under the title "Lack of a Price Mechanism and the Economic Crisis." In this summary, he first reaffirms that the British and German approaches will not solve the problem of unemployment because the labor market will not be in equilibrium unless wages are free to fluctuate. He then warns against the current trend toward a managed economy.

> This conclusion will displease the majority of the public. ...Indeed, fixing wages will allow those workers who are employed to keep a little more money than they would in a system of free competition. But it leaves the rest of the workforce unemployed and unhappy. This unhappiness is only marginally alleviated by unemployment insurance. In addition, it creates a serious crisis. The effects of this crisis will spread gradually and put the entire economic organization at the worst risk (Rueff, 1979, vol. II-2, p. 263).

Partly because of its straightforward title, the 1931 article caused a bigger stir in European countries than the 1925 article. First, *The Times* published a detailed introduction by Josiah Stamp on June 11 and 12, 1931. Then, on June 22, Margaret Bondfield, Minister of Labor in the Ramsay Macdonald Labor Party cabinet, who had read the article, took up the Rueff article in a speech to the House of Commons and accused the anonymous "Frenchman" of slandering the British working class without evidence. The speech inspired a lengthy debate in the House of Commons plenary session, thus Rueff became a household name in London. In addition, economists such as Alexander Loveday and Arthur Cecil Pigou took up Rueff's thesis. Meanwhile, in the French-speaking world, economists began to use the term "Rueff's law" (Rueff, 1977, vol. I, pp. 87–97).

3.2.3 Comments by Keynes and Two Supplements

So, what did Keynes think of the Rueff paper which caused such a stir in the British national debate? As will be discussed in detail in Chap. 4, Rueff had already been in contact with Keynes since the autumn of 1928. After he was appointed as the Financial Officer in London in May 1930, he was invited to the famous "Tuesday Club" dinner and came into close contact with Keynes. On May 16, 1932, Rueff gave a lecture entitled "Political Economy and Economic Policy" at the Arts School in Cambridge under the auspices of the Marshall Society. The exact content of the lecture is not clear, but it seems to have been about the significance of adjustments due to price fluctuations. Keynes and Ralph Hawtrey were present at the event, and the two "made important comments" on the spot (Rueff, 1977, vol. I, p.113). Four days later, on May 20, Keynes sent a letter to Rueff in which he wrote about the lecture.

> I appreciated your talk at Cambridge the other day....I agree with most of your ideas. If there is a difference between us, it is one point. I think that you want the structures to adjust themselves to the original structures, while I want the structures to adjust to the new conditions. I think of it this way. I believe that the flexibility you are counting on is a fantasy, and that we must build a system that can function without relying on flexibility (Lettre de Keynes, cited in Rueff, 1977, vol. I, pp. 104–105).

In short, although Keynes highly praised Rueff at the level of economic theory, he considered the functioning of the price mechanism in markets, especially in the labor market, which Rueff emphasized, to be unrealistic.

Finally, let us make two additional points about Rueff's discussion of the unemployment problem. First, in later years (the late 1950s), the Phillips curve, which shows that there is a trade-off between inflation and unemployment, became known. Rueff clearly stated that this theory is wrong because it does not deal with wages. However, since this theory was developed in the 1950s, when Keynesian theory was dominating the world, it was assumed that (nominal) wages were downwardly rigid. It is possible that this was the reason why wages were not addressed.

Second, Rueff's two articles on unemployment in England are based exclusively on statistical analysis, which gives the impression that he was strict about the problem of unemployment. In later years, he explained this point as follows: Downward adjustment of wages is possible if the imbalances are minor. But if there is a large imbalance, this method cannot be applied from a political and humanitarian point of view. When a major downward adjustment is necessary, his own solution is to devalue the currency to raise domestic prices and lower real wages. The two internationally well-known success stories in which he was involved, the parity calculation of the new franc adopted in 1928 and the formulation of the fiscal consolidation plan in France in December 1958, are based on this very idea (Rueff, 1977, vol. I, p. 102)).

Chapter 4
The German Transfer Controversy

The huge reparation payments that Germany had to make after World War I posed a major problem for international politics and economics. Among other things, it was feared that the conversion of mark funds into foreign currency, the so-called "transfer," associated with the payment of reparations, would threaten the stability of the mark and further aggravate the economic crisis in postwar Germany. For this reason, the Dawes Plan, formulated in 1929, called for reparation payments to be made to the extent that they did not damage the market price of the mark. The "transfer controversy" that developed among economists was also about the same issue. The most famous of these controversies was between Keynes, Rueff, and Bertil Ohlin in 1929 and published in *The Economic Journal* of which Keynes was editor-in-chief.

4.1 Rueff and Keynes in Geneva

In the fall of 1928, during the plenary session of the League of Nations, Rueff and Keynes were invited to the Graduate Institute for Advanced International Studies in Geneva. After giving their reports to graduate students of the institute, they had an open discussion. Paul Manteau, the director of the institute and a great scholar of the history of the Industrial Revolution in England, brought the two intellectuals, who were the talk of the town, together and had them face each other.

Rueff's report was on the transfer issue. When the discussion moved on, Keynes asked Rueff, "By the way, how is this adjustment to be done?" Rueff's answer was this. When the balance of payments is in the red, gold flows out of the country. The outflow of gold immediately means that the purchasing power of the country is transferred to the rest of the world, which in turn reduces domestic demand. As a result, prices will fall, supply will decrease, and equilibrium will eventually be restored. Keynes walked around the stage and listened to Rueff's answer, but suddenly stopped and said, "That's a very interesting idea. I would like to think about it carefully." Rueff recalled that Keynes, from his appearance at that time, did not

Y. Gonjo et al., *The Truth of Liberal Economy*, Springer Studies in the History of Economic Thought, https://doi.org/10.1007/978-981-99-0841-7_4

seem to know the concept of aggregate demand (Rueff, 1967, p. 494). Incidentally, Keynes used this concept in *A Treatise on Money* (Keynes, 1930/1971, vol. V) and *The General Theory of Employment, Interest and Money* (Keynes, 1936/1983, vol.VII). Rueff, on the other hand, had used this concept ahead of Keynes in "A Study of Monetary Phenomena" (*Théorie des phénomènes monétaires*) (Rueff, 1927).

In September 1928, around the time of his encounter with Keynes in Geneva, Rueff published a paper entitled "Economic Fallacies, the Organization of Transfers" (Rueff, 1928/1979, vol. II-2). In this paper, Rueff considers three periods of drastic changes in France's balance of payments: (1) 1908–09, (2) immediately before and after World War I, and (3) 1919–22, and verifies through statistical analysis that even during these periods, the balance of payments was adjusted without problems, and maintained equilibrium. In other words, the movement of gold and foreign currencies was relatively small, and adjustments were made by other balance of payment items, especially the trade balance.

In particular, he examines in detail the adjustment from 1919 to 1922. During the war, France received 170 billion francs in wartime financial assistance from the United Kingdom and the United States. This huge amount of financial assistance covered the large deficit in the trade balance and pegged the franc to the pound and the dollar. However, with the end of the war, this financial assistance was suspended in the first quarter of 1919. Thus, a deficit of 170 billion francs suddenly appeared in France's balance of payments. But there was no imbalance in France's balance of payments. Using the statistical data of France and the United States, Rueff explains the reason for this as follows. The purchasing power of the franc in the United States plummeted after the suspension of financial support, resulting in a sharp increase in exports to the United States and a sharp decrease in imports from the United States, which reduced France's trade deficit with the United States. This is why the balance of payments was balanced. During this period, the exchange rate of the franc against the dollar was stable, so the adjustment was achieved solely through prices. Moreover, the government was not involved in this adjustment.

From this empirical result, Rueff argues as follows: according to the classical theory, adjustment should be made by changes in prices or exchange rates. In the French case, however, the adjustment is made exclusively by changes in prices. Generally speaking, during inflationary periods, adjustment is supposed to be made by prices. Therefore, the adjustment of the balance of payments does not necessarily require exchange rate fluctuations. What has been confirmed for France should also be true for the German transfer problem. Rueff says.

> Contrary to the too prevalent view, there are no obstacles preventing transfers from Germany....The presence or absence of a transfer-enabling instrument at a particular point in time will never constrain the amount of actual transfer. This is because it is always the actual transfer that determines whether a transfer is possible or not. Therefore, interrupting a transfer because the exchange market does not have the necessary means for the transfer is tantamount to deliberately abandoning the only way to make the transfer possible (Rueff, 1928/1979, vol. II-2, pp. 195–196).

Thus, Rueff concludes that "the transfer problem does not exist" and that "what is important is not the transfer problem but the budget problem," that is, the internal political problem of how much the German people can bear the increased tax burden resulting from reparation payments.

Rueff sent the paper to Keynes, who could read French. It was not until later that a debate took place in *The Economic Journal*. The controversy was to take place in the following manner. First, Keynes wrote a paper, which was published in the March issue of 1929. Then, Rueff and Ohlin wrote a critical article on it and sent it to Keynes. Keynes read through the manuscript and wrote a "reply," and the three manuscripts were published in the same journal. The three authors' manuscripts were scheduled to be published in the June issue. However, after reading Keynes's article, Rueff decided to write a new article, "Mr. Keynes's Views on the Transfer Problem," in place of the article he had sent to Keynes earlier. For this reason, the publication of both the Rueff paper and Keynes's "Answer" was postponed to the September issue.

4.2 The Rueff-Keynes Debate—Rueff's Critique of Keynes

First, let's look at Keynes's theory of transfer which went something like this (Keynes, 1983, vol. XI, pp. 451–459).

Most commentators believe that Germany's reparation payments will come down to financial problems. But it is not that simple. As pointed out in the Dawes proposal, in addition to the financial problem, there is the problem of transfers. In order to solve the transfer problem, it is necessary to secure foreign currency by increasing exports from Germany, unless loans are sought from abroad. In order to do this, it is necessary to reduce the cost of production of industrial products, measured in gold. One of the best ways to reduce production costs is to lower wages. But there are several problems with this. First, the German people's spending will be reduced not only by higher taxes to pay for reparations but also by lowering wages. Secondly, deflationary policies could be used to reduce wages, but since deflation creates unemployment, there is the question of whether this is politically and humanely feasible. Furthermore, lowering wages will cause the powerful German industry to compete fiercely with its neighbors, which will strain international economic relations.

By the way, even if the reduction of wages is realized and the international competitiveness of German industry increases, it will not be easy to increase exports. In general, a country's exports are determined by the relationship between the economic structure of the country and the economic structure of its neighbors, and neither of these economic structures can be changed immediately. Therefore, if we take a certain point in time, there is a "natural level" of a country's exports. Keynes said that historically, foreign investment has tended to be adjusted to the trade balance, not the other way around. Incidentally, in his autobiography in 1978, Rueff wrote that the framework of Keynes's thought had already been formed at that time (Rueff, 1977, vol. I, p. 50).

The Keynesian argument logically leads to one solution which is to match the amount of transfers to the level of Germany's trade surplus. Or, to borrow Rueff's term, "organize" transfers.

Next, let's move on to Rueff's criticism of Keynes. Rueff says there are two theoretical errors in Keynes's transfer theory. The first is that Keynes assumed that higher taxes and lower wages would lead to lower spending by the German people. According to Rueff, a reduction in wages should theoretically be linked to a reduction in the prices of all domestic goods by the same percentage. In addition, since the income of the German people obtained by the state through higher taxes is used to buy foreign currency from exporters, the income of these traders will increase. Therefore, the real expenditure of the people as a whole will not decrease.

Another error is Keynes's assumption that there is a "natural level" of exports. Rueff argues that there is no basis for this claim and presents examples that show the smoothness of balance of payments adjustments in France. Most of the examples are ones that he had already written about in his French paper. What is new is the addition of the period from the end of 1923 to the end of 1925. According to Rueff, even though a large amount of capital exports took place in this newly added period, France's balance of payments was balanced without any problem. This is because the trade balance, which had been in deficit, turned into a surplus. "Thus, at all times (after the war), France's balance of trade adapted with remarkable accuracy to changes in the financial components of the balance of payments (first political loans, then foreign investment). This was so despite the fact that these fluctuations were sudden and enormous. These fluctuations had nothing to do with what Keynes called the economic structure of the trading partners" (Rueff, 1979, vol. II-2, p. 209).

Thus, Rueff concludes that there is no transfer problem from either a theoretical or empirical point of view, and that the only problem is the internal political problem of how far the German people can bear the burden of higher taxes. However, he is not satisfied with this conclusion and goes on to say Keynes's questioning of the "*fluidité* of economic phenomena" is significant. It concerns the question of the principle of choosing between a "liberal economy" and an "organized economy," and is "more important from a political point of view than from the point of view of economic theory" since Keynesian thinking "leads inevitably to the practice of an 'organized economy' akin to communism" (Rueff, 1979, vol. II-2, pp. 214–215).

This argument by Rueff seems rather abrupt. However, at that time, a fascist government had already been established in France's neighboring country, Italy, and Hitler was gaining influence in Germany. Furthermore, the Communist Party had won 24 seats in the French National Assembly in the 1924 election. For this reason, the denial of liquidity by Keynes could not have been overlooked by the self-confessed libertarian Rueff.

4.3 The Rueff-Keynes Debate—Keynes's Response

Keynes wrote a thank you letter to Rueff as soon as he received the manuscript of his paper. In the letter, he asked Rueff if he would criticize Keynes for overestimating the delay in the adjustment of wages to prices. Rueff replies to Keynes: "It is not that I am overestimating. In the past, large adjustments have been made to prices without major problems. In the light of this experience, I am saying that the same will be true in the future" (de Rueff à Keynes, cited in Rueff, vol. I, 1977, p. 50).

Keynes refutes Rueff in his "Reply by Mr. Keynes" published in *The Economic Journal.* It is divided into three points (Keynes, 1929/1983, vol. XI, pp. 475–480). First, it focuses on the meaning of the term "decline in German national spending." According to Keynes, it means that if wages are lowered, Germany's terms of trade will worsen, and the real purchasing power of the German people will decrease. Therefore, according to Keynes, the first criticism from Rueff is based on a misunderstanding and is not valid. His second point regards the effectiveness of adjustment by the price mechanism, which Rueff relies upon. In the case of Germany, since the problem is the reduction of real wages, adjustment "would be politically and humanely difficult, if not impossible."

Thirdly, Keynes questions Rueff's example of the French balance of payments adjustment. Keynes draws on the example of the stabilization of the franc in France in 1928, i.e., the devaluation of the gold parity of the franc to one-fifth of its pre-war level. This devaluation caused "severe social disruptions, massive redistribution of wealth, and the mass destruction of existing contracts," thus, it is hard to say, accordingly, that the adjustment was smooth in France. And Keynes is no less vehement than Rueff in his words. "How forgetful of Mr. Rueff, himself a Frenchman, to cite France's postwar economic history to prove that economic adjustment is as easy as peeling a pea pod!" (Keynes, 1929/1983, vol. XI, p. 477).[1]

Keynes's "answer" gives us an idea of the characteristics of his transfer theory and (or) its problems. The core of his theory of transfer lies in the fact that he sees the adjustment of the economy according to the classical theory, that is, as "difficult, if not impossible." This is because he believes that in order to transfer a huge amount of purchasing power out of the country to pay for reparations, not only will taxes have to be raised but also wages will have to be lowered.

This Keynesian argument, when placed within the framework of Rueff's argument, becomes the following, which completely changes its meaning. If purchasing power is transferred out of the country as a result of reparation payments, the purchasing power of the mark in other countries will fall. As a result, exports increase and imports decrease, and the trade balance deficit decreases (or surplus increases). Thus, the balance of payments is balanced. In other words, Rueff sees the decline in the purchasing power of the mark in other countries as a kind of price mechanism, a factor that brings about equilibrium, while Keynes sees as a deterioration in the terms of trade resulting from a reduction in wages (a factor that brings about a decline in the standard of living of the people). Incidentally, for Rueff, large-scale adjustments due to fluctuations in the purchasing power of currencies among nations—fluctuations in the "divergence" of currencies in Rueff's terminology—are nothing special, as France has experienced them many times since the nineteenth century.

[1] The final part of Keynes' reply is debatable. Keynes, in his article written in 1928, highly appraised the stabilization of the franc, especially the new parity avoiding deflation. Keynes, however, in those days had no way to know the fact that the new parity of the franc was calculated by Rueff. Keynes' evaluation of the franc stabilization is contradictory between these two articles.

Interestingly, in his "answer" Keynes does not mention at all the "natural level" of exports, which Rueff persistently rejected with many examples. If he were to retract this, he would be forced to admit that the balance of payments is adjusted by changes in the balance of trade, which he insists upon, and this would destroy the pillar of his transfer theory. Likewise, Keynes does not mention Rueff's criticism that we will end up with an "organized economy" similar to communism. In order to refute this criticism, it is necessary to go into the meaning of freedom at the individual level and therefore also of coordination at the microeconomic level. Was it to avoid this? The truth is not clear. Perhaps the originality of Keynes's thought lies in the fact that he avoided answering these two criticisms.

The Rueff-Keynes controversy shows that there is a crucial difference in the placement of the interests of the two economic theorists. Keynes prioritizes the avoidance of the political and humanitarian hardship of impoverishing the German people by lowering wages and rejects adjustment through the price mechanism. Therefore, it is clear that his concern is short-term, and his theory of transfer has a strong chronological character. On the other hand, however, since Keynes believed that there is a "natural level" of exports, it can be thought that he was trying to present his transfer theory as a general theory.

In contrast, Rueff limits his discussion to theory and evidence and emphasizes the effectiveness of coordination. This approach is clearly the very one he developed in his philosophical work ("From Physical to Moral Sciences"). In relation to the political and humanitarian aspects of Keynes's problem, it can be said that Rueff was more concerned with the higher-order, medium- to long-term problem of preventing the emergence of an "organized economy" that deprives people of their freedom. Incidentally, it was not until he launched neoliberalism at the end of the 1930s that Rueff began to address the political and humanitarian issues raised by Keynes, based on the premise of the effectiveness of adjustment. We shall return to this in Chap. 9.

In general, in English-speaking publications, the transfer controversy is presented as the Keynes/Ohlin controversy. It is not clear why Rueff has been omitted from this controversy. It may be that Rueff's emphasis on empirical evidence meant that his papers were seen as not contributing to theoretical research. However, according to Rueff's scientific methodology, a theory is meaningful only when it is supported by empirical evidence, and a theory that is at odds with empirical results cannot be a theory. Since he had already proven that the classical theory of balance of payments was theoretically valid through his theoretical research, he thought that the role he should play was to verify the theory through empirical evidence. This is evident in Rueff's reply to Keynes's letter introduced at the beginning of this section.

Nevertheless, from a long-term perspective, the Rueff-Keynes controversy has an extremely important meaning for the social sciences in the twentieth century. This is because there is already a clear, albeit nascent, social philosophical opposition between Keynesianism and neoliberalism that goes beyond the framework of economics in the narrow sense. It is also worth noting that Rueff's argument was based not only on theory but also on the first empirical study of the balance of payments in Europe and the United States, mainly in France.

Chapter 5
The Reconstructed International Monetary System and the Process of Its Collapse—Rueff, the Unwavering Theorist

The period between the two world wars was a time of turmoil and confusion in terms of politics, economics, and society. Rueff in those days was at the forefront of tense domestic and international monetary issues, confronting the harsh realities of the time in the following functions: member of the Financial Committee of the League of Nations, then Financial Commissioner in London, then Deputy Director General of the Treasury Department, then Director General of the Treasury Department, and finally Deputy Governor of the Bank of France. During this period, he continued his research in economics and its adjacent sciences and developed into a leading theorist of classical economics as well as a theorist of neoliberalism.

After World War II, he made bold proposals for reform of the crisis-ridden French economy and the international monetary system and became known throughout the world as an active economist. What supported him in the latter half of his life was his economics, which he refined through theoretical research and practical experience during the interwar period. In this chapter, we shall examine the actions and discourse of Rueff, as both a practitioner and an economic theorist, placing them in the context of the times.

5.1 The Gold Exchange Standard

The restoration of the gold standard, which had been suspended at the outbreak of World War I, was one of the most important postwar tasks for countries. Restoring the convertibility of the national currencies with gold was seen as essential both to ending the inflation that countries suffered after the war and to reviving international trade. However, the situation surrounding the gold standard had changed dramatically. World prices were 50% higher than they had been before the war, but the supply of gold was not increasing at a corresponding rate. Moreover, most of the gold was concentrated in the United States, which had become the world's largest creditor nation, and the United States kept its dollar gold parity unchanged. It was clear

Y. Gonjo et al., *The Truth of Liberal Economy*, Springer Studies in the History of Economic Thought, https://doi.org/10.1007/978-981-99-0841-7_5

that there would be a shortage of gold if each country tried to restore the full gold standard to what it had been before the war. This led to the creation of the gold exchange standard.

The gold exchange standard is a system of issuing a country's currency using the national currency of a major power as a reserve, which is guaranteed to be exchanged for gold. In 1922, at the Genoa Conference held under the auspices of the League of Nations, a resolution was passed at the initiative of the United Kingdom, recommending that the shortage of gold be made up by external balances. Based on this resolution, the gold exchange standard was introduced to Eastern European countries under the guidance of the League of Nations Monetary Committee. At first, the Genoa Resolution did not cause any problems. However, as soon as the return of Britain, Germany, and France to the gold standard was on the agenda, it became a major political issue. The United Kingdom strongly urged the three countries to adopt a gold exchange standard using the pound sterling and the dollar as reserves because of the shortage of gold that would result if Germany and France returned to the gold standard. France rejected the Bank of England's demand, saying that it would be "imperialistic" to issue a currency based on the pound sterling, the national currency of the United Kingdom, which had returned to the gold standard.

In reality, however, France acceded to British demands and, like Germany, remained on a de facto gold exchange standard until September 1931, when Britain left the gold standard. Thirty to fifty percent of the Bank of France's reserves were transferred to the French government and placed in the London and New York markets in the form of deposits or Treasury bills, or pound and dollar balances (Gonjo, 1999, p.30,78). Every morning in London, it was Rueff, the resident treasurer in London, who called all the banks in the city to check their interest rates and manage the French government's pound sterling funds. Since the funds managed by Rueff were equivalent to 10% of the total deposits in London, it is said that there was not a banker in the region who did not know his name (Rueff, 1967, p. 500).

The policies implemented under the reconstructed international monetary system were also very different from those before the Great War. The two major powers, Britain and the United States, deviated from the rules of the classical gold standard in their policies. The United States, fearing that the massive influx of gold would lead to inflation in the country, tried to curb the progress of inflation by issuing gold certificates guaranteed by 100% in gold. This was the so-called "gold sterilization policy." In the United Kingdom, the Bank of England began to neutralize the impact of gold outflows on the domestic economy by substituting open market operations for the manipulation of official interest rates, which had been the traditional means of central bank intervention. In order to support sluggish domestic industry, the bank implemented a policy of fixing the official rate at a low level, on the one hand, and increasing the supply of money through open market purchases, on the other. The philosophy behind this policy soon took on an official character in the United Kingdom. In 1931, a report by the committee commonly known as the Macmillan Committee, which was set up within the British Treasury, stated that the ultimate goal of monetary policy should be to stabilize prices and promote exports and employment, and proposed that currency issuance be separated from gold reserves. Keynes often led the discussions in this committee (Committee on Finance and Industry, 1931).

The policies adopted by the United Kingdom and the United States were characterized by the artificial manipulation of the international movement of gold, which limited the automatic adjustment function of the gold standard. The goal of these policies was to achieve price stability, not currency stability, and to achieve inward equilibrium, not outward equilibrium. If the monetary authorities of each country were to control the workings of the gold standard, international friction and conflict would arise. How can such a situation be avoided or resolved? The only way is through "central bank cooperation," that is, coordination among central banks. Since the United States did not join the League of Nations, the Bank of England remained effectively in charge of such coordination. This is how the French Ministry of Finance interpreted the political implications of the actions of Britain and the Bank of England after the Genoa Conference. From the end of the 1920s to the mid-1930s, France was thoroughly opposed to the management of the gold standard. It repelled pressure from the Bank of England to return to the gold standard, which, as mentioned above, was in fact the gold exchange standard. Again there was a political decision not to allow the Bank of England to become "imperialistic."

Throughout the series of events described above, the two principles that underpinned the classical gold standard were the issuance of gold-based currency and the free international movement of gold. The question was whether this principle should be retained or whether, in order to increase the freedom of economic policy, the issuance of currency should be unconstrained by gold and the international movement of gold should be left in the control of the monetary authorities. France (and the Latin countries) stood on the side of the former, that is, "monetary orthodoxy" in the terminology of the time, while the United Kingdom and the United States stood on the side of the latter, a "modified gold standard" or "managed gold standard." In terms of theory, Rueff was the pillar of the former, and Keynes was the pillar of the latter. However, neither Rueff nor Keynes ever fought on the stage of history over this issue.

In any case, even though the international monetary system had been rebuilt, the system itself and its operation were very different from those before the Great War, and there were serious tensions within this system.

5.2 The Anglo-French "Gold Conference"

Tensions between France and Britain gradually increased from 1926 when France decided to return to the gold standard. France began buying pound sterling exchange to return to the gold standard which then put potential pressure on the pound. In 1928, a new gold parity for the franc was established based on the research and studies of the young financial inspector, Rueff. The new franc (Poincaré franc) was somewhat cheaper than the real franc and helped to boost French exports and stabilize the country's finances which had been in turmoil after the war. As a result, the franc was regarded as the safest currency in the world, and the transfer of funds in pounds sterling from London to Paris via credit increased, accelerating the outflow of gold to Paris. The outflow of gold surged from the end of 1929, when the effects of the Great Depression began to be felt in European countries. In July 1930, Paris experienced its first gold rush, and from then on, the British media were quick to accuse France of absorbing and storing the world's gold.

From January to February of 1930, three rounds of talks were held in Paris between British and French financial officials to resolve the crisis over the pound. In the run-up to these talks which were commonly referred to as the "Gold Conference" (Gonjo, 1999, pp. 39–48), it was Rueff, the finance officer stationed in London, who gathered and analyzed information in London and advised the head office in Paris on what France should do. In those days, he frequently sent long memoranda to the Ministry in which he analyzed the disputes that arose between the two countries. At the same time, as we will see in more detail in a later section of this book, Rueff examined the balance of payments aspects of the inflow of gold into France and drew the remarkable conclusion that it stemmed from the mechanism of the gold exchange standard. At the Gold Conference, however, he was not only an economic theorist but also a financial bureaucrat representing the national interest. It went something like this.

British financial officials saw the concentration of gold in Paris as a result of the "inelasticity" of the French financial system and called for France to make the system more flexible. They were particularly concerned about the fact that the Bank of France was not allowed to operate on the open market, and they wanted the French government to take two actions. First, the system should be reformed to allow the Bank of France to freely intervene in the open market. Second, the Bank of France should conduct massive buying operations to lower the market interest rate in Paris and encourage the outflow of gold from Paris to the rest of the world.

Rueff dismissed these British claims as misguided. According to him, there were two reasons for the outflow of gold from London. The first was the Bank of England's low-interest rate policy. If the Bank of England had stopped this policy and kept the market interest rate in London somewhat higher than in Paris, the outflow of gold from London to Paris would stop. However, the consequence of such a strategy would be that the demand for credit that had been gathering in London would move to Paris, and London would lose its position as the world's financial center. In fact, in an attempt to avoid such a situation, the United Kingdom was "asking France to take measures that would allow it to avoid imposing the credit restrictions necessary to defend its currency." Another cause was the unemployment insurance system. With this system, Rueff claimed, Britain "fixed wages at a level which is absolutely invariable and independent of all fluctuations in the general price level" resulting in the British industry losing its market and going into recession.[1]

As for the open market operation, which was the focus of the British demand, Rueff rejected the demand in strong terms. He reported this exchange with Ralph Hawtrey, Assistant Secretary of the Treasury in London, as follows:

[1] Archives économiques et financières (AEF), B31851, note de Rueff, 17 février 1931.

> The British reply to our answer is basically based on the following argument. There is a very inadequate amount of rediscountable stock [securities] on the Paris market. Therefore, the only way to unlock gold is to replace the borrowed gold stock of the Bank of France with other assets – in effect, government bonds. I advised him that it comes down to the much-feared and [in fact] very frightening policy of issuing securities [government bonds] that guarantee the credit of the nation. He said that both the U.S. and the U.K. were doing so. I advised him categorically that your idea would put the entire policy of the correspondent banks, especially the automaticity – which seems to me to be the only safeguard against error – in question.[2]

The above analysis by Rueff was shared by the French Ministry of Finance and the Bank of France. Thus, the root of the Anglo-French conflict over gold was at the level of principle, whether to accept or reject the automatic adjustment function of the gold standard. At the same time, the conflict also involved a political feud between Britain and France over whether to allow Paris to replace London as the international financial center or to prevent it from doing so.

The gap between the French and the British was so great that the two countries could not come to an agreement at the negotiations held in Paris. In the end, the outflow of gold from Britain did not stop, and the country left the gold standard in September 1931. This caused the pound to depreciate by 25–30% in one fell swoop, which in turn caused the price of raw materials to plummet around the world. Deflation spread around the world, and the recession became globalized at once.

5.3 The Great Depression of the 1930s and the International Monetary System Problem

How the Great Recession Was Caused by the Gold Exchange Standard

In a memorandum to the Minister of Finance in October 1931, shortly after Britain left the gold standard, Rueff tried to theorize about the causes of the global recession.

He begins by asserting that, from a monetary point of view, the recession is "largely the fault of the international monetary system known as the gold exchange standard, which was introduced in a number of European countries at the behest of the Monetary Committee of the League of Nations." He then analyzes the workings of the gold exchange standard and shows that there are serious risks involved in this monetary system. A similar analysis was made in a lecture he gave in Paris in March 1932, which was published in the *Revue des Deux Mondes* that April and was included in a collection of lectures published the same year (Rueff, 1932; Rueff, 1971, pp. 14–18). The following is a summary of the argument that Rueff developed there.

Under the gold exchange standard, central banks are allowed to hold foreign currencies (dollars and pounds) that flow into their country via credit, in addition to claims denominated in their own currency. This foreign currency is transferred to

[2] AEF, Note de Jacques Rueff, 5 février 1931; Gonjo, 1999, pp. 44–45.

the central bank's reserves, but the currency itself is sent to New York and London, where much of it is deposited in local financial institutions. Therefore, the United States and United Kingdom can lend the same currency out again. Since the lent currency returns to New York and London as deposits, both countries can lend the same currency to foreign countries again and again. Rueff describes these loaned dollars and pounds as "like soldiers appearing repeatedly on the stage of a comedy play" (Rueff, 1971, p. 17). Incidentally, as mentioned in the previous section, Rueff was the city's resident treasurer in London at the time and was responsible for the management and operation of this deposit (the London Balance).

Thus, capital lent by the United States and the United Kingdom is deposited in both countries to prepare for new credit creation, so that the aggregate purchasing power of the two countries is not reduced. In fact, the opposite is true. As the amount and frequency of foreign lending increase, the volume of deposits in the New York and London markets increases, and so does credit creation. Therefore, the total purchasing power of both these countries will increase. On the other hand, liquidity increases in countries that receive capital from the United States and United Kingdom, also increasing their purchasing power.

Thus, according to Rueff, the gold exchange standard is "a terrible inflationary device" (Rueff, 1971, p. 18). He contends that the gold exchange standard was the monetary cause of the global boom on the eve of the depression of 1929, and the international monetary system that collapsed in the 1930s was not a gold standard but a gold exchange standard.

In the aftermath of World War II, Rueff's original diagnosis of the crisis of the dollar and the international monetary system drew the attention of the world. The mechanism of the gold exchange standard, which he discovered in the early 1930s, provided the theoretical basis for his argument.

France's Isolation and the Collapse of Monetary Orthodoxy

As mentioned earlier, deflation became a global phenomenon when the United Kingdom left the gold standard. The United States was particularly affected by this. This was because the price of agricultural products plummeted, making it impossible for the country's farmers to repay the huge debts they had incurred. In April 1933, U.S. President Franklin Roosevelt suspended the gold standard in order to raise domestic prices. A month later, the World Economic Conference was held in London with the aim of rebuilding the world economy, but this conference also ended in failure. At this time, France formed a gold bloc with neighboring Latin countries to defend the gold standard. However, this forced France to strengthen its protectionist trade and deflationary policies. The country's political will to stay on the gold standard was clearly at odds with the economic policies it adopted. The defense of the gold standard was in name only.

The situation changed dramatically in February 1934 when the United States resumed gold purchases at a new official rate of $35 per ounce of gold. The currencies of the gold bloc countries became the target of international speculation, and large amounts of gold began to flow out of these countries. The reason for this was the currency wars between Britain and the United States, described as follows: The

United States does not want the dollar to rise, which would be detrimental to the recovery of domestic prices, while the United Kingdom tries to keep the pound in its "natural state" and prevent it from rising. As a result, the British Exchange Equilibrium Account and the U.S. Exchange Stabilization Fund intervene in the market from opposite directions. This is a currency war. Since the currencies of the gold bloc countries were bound to the dollar in gold, each time the British Equilibrium Account intervened, the gold-denominated price of exports from the pound zone fell. As a result, the gold bloc countries' trade deficit with the pound widened, the balance of payments imbalance widened, and gold flowed out.

Since the United States resumed its gold purchases, the franc played only a minor role between the two major currencies, the dollar and the pound. The currency war between the UK and the United States is bound to continue as long as prices do not enter a rising phase in the United States and France, in the meantime, has no choice but to wait for prices to rise in the United States while maintaining its protectionist trade and deflationary policies. However, by 1935, the deflationary policy in France itself was nearing its limit. The country no longer had any policy options other than devaluation of the franc or exchange control.

At the time, Rueff was the deputy director for international finance in the Treasury Department, and he too felt that the devaluation of the franc was unavoidable. The monetary orthodoxy on which France and Rueff had relied had effectively collapsed. However, since French national opinion was still firmly united in maintaining the gold standard, the government of the day (a centrist government) could not devalue the franc. Military tensions were rising between France and Hitler's Germany, and in the event of war, it would be necessary to seek massive financial support from Britain and the United States, which both had free exchange systems, as was the case during World War I.

What changed the stalemate was the political action of workers, especially organized labor, and the change in political power. As deflation worsened, the People's Front movement, with its banner of anti-depression and anti-fascism, spread among workers and intellectuals, and became a major political force. The People's Front won the general election held in May 1936, and a left-wing government headed by Leon Blum, the leader of the Socialist Party, was born (Gonjo, 1999, pp. 48–70).

Suspension of the Gold Standard and Rueff's Action as Director General of the Treasury

After the People's Front won the general election, general strikes and factory occupations by workers spread throughout France. The Blum administration came into power in the midst of this tumultuous situation. As a result, the government was forced to implement policies that took into consideration the workers and farmers suffering from the effects of deflation. These policies would require massive fiscal spending, making it difficult to maintain the gold standard. Going off the gold standard, however, would cause a rift in political relations with both Britain and the United States. The People's Front government found itself in a serious dilemma as soon as it was established.

The government, however, succeeded in escaping this dilemma by concluding a currency agreement among Britain, the United States, and France and devaluing the franc within the framework of this agreement. The trilateral currency agreement was signed in September 1936, and the franc was accordingly devalued in October of the following year. At the same time, France suspended the gold standard. This was followed by the creation of the Exchange Stabilization Fund, which intervened in the market to stabilize the franc exchange rate.

In June 1938, a new law was enacted that added open market operations to the operations of the Bank of France, a policy measure that had been severely criticized by Rueff at the Anglo-French "Gold Conference" in 1930. However, the law included a clause stating that "these operations may not be carried out for the benefit of the treasury or the monetary authority." Rueff, who was a legal director of the Bank of France, also said at a meeting of the Bank's board of directors that "open market policies must always be implemented in an unpopular way" so that buying operations do not encourage the issuance of government bonds and thus create inflation (Gonjo, 1999, pp. 48–70). In other words, open market operations can be used as a means of austerity policy, but not as a means of monetary easing. Thus, even though the new law was enacted, the principal position of the French government and Rueff remained unchanged.

Nevertheless, it is clear that the French government's position and Rueff's claims as an economic theorist that the gold standard was the only currency system that should exist were overcome by a series of new realities after 1931, and both the government and Rueff were forced to adapt to these realities.

It is worth pointing out that Rueff had been appointed Director General of the Treasury Department in November 1936. The Director General of the Treasury is the person who has the highest practical responsibility for economic and financial management in France. No matter how good an economic theorist and capable a bureaucrat Rueff was, the fact that a left-wing government appointed him to such a key position is disconcerting, and all the more so considering the state of the French economy and society at the time, as well as Rueff's opinions and actions.

The economic and social situation in France at that time was a difficult one. Since the beginning of the 1930s, France had seen a rapid increase in the organization of the economy and society, especially in the various occupational groups represented by labor unions and employers' organizations. At the same time, the social and political influence of these organizations had increased significantly. In a report on a bill presented to the Chamber of Deputies in March 1935, the following statement was made "The reality in France today is one of corporatism. It is *Syndicat*. It is a force with a life of its own….".[3] In line with this evolution toward a corporatist society, "the death of liberalism" and "the end of liberalism" were openly talked about in France, and liberalists were receding into the minority.

Even in the midst of all this, however, Rueff took every opportunity to give lectures extolling economic liberalism and indirectly criticizing the government's protectionist policies. When he gave a lecture at the "University for Peace" in the Sorbonne

[3] Journal official, Doc. Parl. Chambre des députés, no. 3813, 5 juillet 1934.

in February 1933, the Minister of Agriculture went so far as to distribute a letter to the Prime Minister and other ministers calling for his dismissal (Rueff, 1977, vol. I, p. 114).

Why, then, did the Blum government place the self-confessed "non-conformist" Rueff in the position of Director General of the Treasury? There are a number of possible reasons, but the short answer is this. As the government is said to have been influenced by the New Deal in the United States, its policies were basically interventionist policies based on liberalism. In addition, the government emphasized diplomatic relations with Britain and the United States. As military tensions with neighboring Germany were growing by the day, France could not afford to close its borders to Britain and the United States in terms of both economy and currency. In short, due to the nature of the Popular Front government and France's international position, ideological differences had only a secondary influence on the appointment of the head of the Treasury Department.

However, during his time as Director General of the Treasury, Rueff did not achieve anything that would make his mark on history. While maintaining an open economy, the government pursued economic policies that took into account the needs of workers and peasants (wage increases, purchase of wheat with public funds, etc.) and rearmament policies, which led to a large budget deficit and severe inflation as early as 1937. As the daily budget expenditure exceeded the tax revenue, the finance bureau was overwhelmed with cash flow. Whenever there was a cash crunch, the government would borrow from the central bank to make up for it. Against the backdrop of this critical financial situation, speculative capital had been pouring out of the country. For this reason, the franc was devalued twice more before the start of World War II.

His primary responsibility was to present the government with policy options whenever there was a revenue shortfall. However, each of the options he presented was only a temporary postponement of the catastrophe. In later years, Rueff recalled the time and said roughly as follows: that the stumbling block for the People's Front government was its inability to prepare an "overall plan" to finally bring the budget balance into balance. The fiscal reform plan Rueff drew up under President de Gaulle in 1958, which was so successful that it was described as a "miracle," was, according to Rueff, informed by his bitter experience during the Popular Front period.

In concluding this chapter, I would like to emphasize three issues relevant to the chapters that follow.

First, Rueff's theoretical argument for a gold standard was ultimately buried by the actions of organized labor in France and the policy choices of the leftist government. The importance of society and politics for economics had already been emphasized by Keynes in the transfer debate. It was only in 1936 that Rueff came to first understand the weight of the issues raised by Keynes.

Secondly, this did not in any way shake his basic position that micro-adjustment should be at the core of theory and policy theory as will become clear in Chap. 6.

Thirdly, during his tenure as Director General of the Treasury, Rueff shifted the research interests in two interrelated directions. The first issue involves a shift of focus in his research from monetary theory to social philosophy, which came to fruition in his major work, "Social Order," in 1945. The second issue would lead to his formulating and defining a form of liberalism that could respond to the realities of the twentieth century (especially the demand movement of organized labor), taking into account short-term needs as well as Keynes did. The results of this appeared as early as 1938 in the form of the theory of "neoliberalism." Within the framework of this redefined liberalism, Rueff pursues a form of state intervention that is compatible with the price mechanism. To borrow Rueff's metaphor, it is the development of technology to fly an airplane in the presence of gravity.

Chapter 6
Keynes's "General Theory" Which is not a General Theory

In 1936, Keynes published *The General Theory of Employment, Interest and Money*. At the time, Rueff was in a key position as Director General of the Treasury Department of the Ministry of Finance and was busy managing the tight finances under the Popular Front government. He was finally relieved of the drudgery of his post in September 1939. However, this was short-lived, as France was defeated by Germany in the early stages of World War II, and he was forced to resign his official position and retreat to a small village. During the four and a half years of the German occupation, he devoted his unfortunate days to writing his life's work, "Social Order," which was published as a two-volume magnum opus in 1945.

It was not until 1947, when the postwar turmoil was beginning to subside, that Rueff was able to face "the General Theory" squarely. By this time, according to Rueff, Keynesian theory had become the "bible" of the postwar West (except for West Germany), and all policymakers had been converted to this "religion." In these countries, full employment was the central goal of postwar policy, based on Keynesian theory. The United Nations also created the Economic and Employment Commission. Rueff was sent as a representative of the French government to this commission which was dominated by Keynesian enthusiasts.

In France, the French translation of the "General Theory" was published in 1942, and Keynesian theory was already well known among the bureaucrats of the Vichy government and activists of the resistance movement during the war. When the war ended and reconstruction became a top policy priority, the theory was treated as a savior by economic and financial bureaucrats and economists. A number of documents show the enthusiasm of the time. In March 1945, François Perroux, a leading figure in the postwar world of French economists, gave a report on Keynesian theory at a study group. The manuscript of the presentation was delivered to the Treasury Department of the Ministry of Finance and the General Affairs Department of the Bank of France. "Keynesian theory, which has a very wide range of applications, has not yet taken root in French economic thought. … classical theory is of no use in an underemployed economy [such as postwar France]. Keynesian theory, on the

Y. Gonjo et al., *The Truth of Liberal Economy*, Springer Studies in the History of Economic Thought, https://doi.org/10.1007/978-981-99-0841-7_6

contrary, is a theory of development, growth, and economic boom."[1]It is important to note that Keynesian theory was already understood not only as a theory of employment, but also as a theory of "development, growth, and economic boom."

In early 1947, Rueff published an article, "The Fallacies of Lord Keynes's General Theory," in the French Journal of Political Economy in defiance of the current trend toward Keynesianism (Rueff, 1947/1979, vol. II-2). Keynes had died the year before, and the opportunity for his own reply had already been lost. Instead, it was the spirited Keynesian James Tobin who attempted to comment on the Rueff paper.

6.1 The Fallacy of Lord Keynes's General Theory

Ignoring the "Monetary Adjustment Phenomenon"

Rueff's criticisms of the General Theory cover a wide range of topics, but there are three main ones. The central criticism is that Keynes ignores the "monetary adjustment phenomenon" or the "money adjustment mechanism." As will be discussed further, the adjustment phenomenon of money is a mechanism by which the total of demand expressed in money (aggregate demand) is adjusted to the total of supply expressed in money (aggregate supply) through changes in prices, interest rates, and exchange rates, in order to establish equilibrium. This is in line with Jean-Baptiste Say's theory of the sales channel. According to Rueff, this is the "corner stone of the whole monetary theory." In "The Theory of Monetary Phenomena," which he published in 1952, he had verified, from both theoretical and empirical perspectives, the existence of such a rigorous law comparable to the laws of physics. He further refined this theory in the aforementioned "Social Order" and positioned it as the cornerstone of his own economics.

Keynes briefly summarized his theory in the third chapter of the "Introduction" to his "General Theory." Rueff quotes excerpts from this section and summarizes Keynes's theory as follows: "Keynes's analysis relies entirely on the psychological hypothesis of the inadequate propensity of production workers to consume. According to this hypothesis, an increase in income resulting from an increase in employment will increase the demand for consumer goods by no more than the amount of the increase. If income does not generate demand for consumer goods, and the government does not spend the same amount on investment as it does on income, then there will be no buyers for the increase in production resulting from increased employment. Since both...production and the income that enables its purchase are limited, equilibrium is established with underemployment" (Rueff, 1979, vol. II-2, p. 275).

Rueff dismisses this Keynesian analysis as a fallacy. Here is why. Even if a worker who benefits from increased employment spends only a portion of his increased

---

[1] Archives de la Banque de France, ISEA, note no.1: Henri Bertoli, *Financement de la reprise*.

income on the purchase of consumer goods, he acquires money instead. This additional demand for cash will be adjusted through the price mechanism and transformed into a demand for consumption and investment goods. In other words, the money in the hands of the worker is not withdrawn due to a preference for liquidity, as Keynes said. Thus, since the additional demand for cash forms a sales channel for labor, underemployment will not persist.

The question then becomes the mechanism of adjustment by price. In order to make his point clear, Rueff first takes the example of a society in which only gold is used as money. When employment increases in such a society, the "cash on hand" of the workers who benefit from it increases. Here, cash on hand refers to the money, i.e., cash and bank balances (M1 in today's terminology), that individuals (ordinary people and companies) keep on hand to continue their daily lives or business activities (Rueff, 1977, vol. I, p. 191).

If all conditions remain the same, most notably the amount of cash on hand desired by the other members of society, the increase in the cash on hand of the worker will cause the cash on hand of the other members of society to decrease. In order to bring their cash on hand back to the previous level, there is no choice but to supply goods unilaterally to the market. As the supply of goods increases, prices will fall. Only the price of gold does not fluctuate because gold is used as money in this society and is purchased at parity by the central bank. As a result, the productive capacity allocated to the production of goods whose prices have fallen is shifted to the production of goods whose prices have not changed, namely gold. As a result, the production of goods other than gold shrinks, and the production of gold expands. Through the mechanism described above, prices will return to their original levels, and the relationship between the price of gold and the market prices of other goods will also return to normal. Thus, employment growth will not be hampered by a lack of demand for investment and production goods.

Next, Rueff considers a society with a general monetary system (i.e., fiat money system, precious metal standard, and a system in which currency is issued via discounted commercial bills). In this case, too, as the cash on hand of workers increases, the cash on hand of others decreases. The latter will sell their goods and credits to restore their own cash on hand to its original level. This causes general prices to fall and interest rates to rise. What is important here is the fact that the fall in prices and the rise in interest rates are inextricably linked. This is because when prices rise, the following arbitrage takes place. First, more people will buy goods in the cash market and sell them in the futures market. As a result, bills are drawn and demand for their discounting increases, causing market interest rates to rise. The market interest rate eventually exceeds the central bank's discount rate (official rate). As a result, bills are brought to the central bank for discounting, and currency issuance increases. This increased issuance of money creates sales channels for the additional goods produced. Thus, under a general monetary system, the same basic mechanism is at work, with the difference that adjustment is somewhat more complicated because it is based on changes in prices and interest rates.

According to Rueff's argument above, when the demand for money increases, the supply of currency increases due to the phenomenon of money adjustment, and the aggregate demand for currency and the aggregate supply of currency are supposed to coincide. However, this assumes that the supply of currency is determined by the demand for cash on hand. Since it is up to the individual, and not the public, to decide how to spend the cash on hand, the dynamism of the economy depends on the behavior of the individual with respect to the cash on hand, that is, it depends on micro-level adjustments.

Furthermore, Rueff says that the mechanism of adjustment is not simply true in theory but can be confirmed under almost all economic systems that existed before the Great War. According to him, prices fluctuate autonomously, effectively affecting the allocation of factors of production. For instance, there was a large difference in gold production between the boom-and-bust periods, which eloquently illustrates the high sensitivity of the production apparatus to price fluctuations.

Why Was the "Monetary Adjustment Phenomenon" Ignored?

So why did Keynes make the mistake of ignoring the phenomenon of monetary adjustment? Rueff identifies two fundamental causes. The first is that Keynes was influenced by the nominal theory of money. For Keynes, "money and credits are empty tokens of value," and "to save is to demand nothing." However, according to Rueff, accumulating money and claims is "to demand the value that money and claims represent," and "to reduce cash holdings is to give up that value, that is, to release it into the market." Therefore, Keynes ignores the "adjustment phenomenon, which is an essential and indispensable phenomenon for the understanding of the price mechanism."

The other reason is that Keynes did not realize that there is a special relationship between the total amount of cash on hand of one individual and the amount of currency in circulation on the other. Rueff explains how he differs with Keynes over this issue as follows. In Keynesian theory, "the quantity of currency created by the banking system is a given, to which the total amount of cash on hand by individuals is [unilaterally] adapted. The amount of currency in circulation is a given that is freely determined by the monetary authorities, without regard to market demand." However, Rueff says: "I am convinced that, on the contrary, it is the amount of cash on hand that individuals want that determines the amount of currency in circulation through the adjustment mechanism" (Rueff, 1979, vol. II-2, p. 288).[2]

To reinforce his point, Rueff asks: "How many people today who have thought long and hard about monetary issues believe that the central bank determines the amount of currency in circulation? Anyone who has been involved with the operations of a central bank, from near or far, with eyes wide open, knows that the amount of currency in circulation cannot be directly changed, even if interest rates are lowered by open market operations." Thus, he concludes: "It seems to me that the fundamental error of Lord Keynes stems from a completely superficial understanding of the monetary mechanism" (Rueff, 1979, vol. II-2, p. 289). In a later speech to the French Ministry

[2] Rueff reinforced his theory in the following article, arguing the adjustment mechanism of money from theory and practice. Rueff, "Eléments pour une théorie du taux d'escompte et de la balance des comptes", *Revue économique*, 8 juillet 1957, repris dans Rueff, 1979, vol. II-2.

of Finance (April 1972), Rueff discussed Milton Friedman's monetarism and again emphasized that "the money supply is not something that can be managed directly."[3]

As the head of the Finance Ministry's Treasury Department under the Popular Front regime, Rueff fought the severe financial crisis and inflation at his own risk. While deputy governor of the Bank of France during the outbreak of war with Germany, the demand for cash exploded, and the bank was faced with a crisis situation where it even had to consider closing its teller windows due to a shortage of cash. Unlike British and American economists, who had never experienced serious inflation in the modern era, Rueff believed that the amount of currency in circulation was unmanageable. His conviction was thus based not only on theory but on his own personal history and practical experience.[4]

Anyway, if we accept the existence of the adjustment mechanism of money, equilibrium cannot be established with underemployment, and Keynesian theory collapses. This is Rueff's first criticism of the "General Theory."

A Blocked Economy, and the Creation of Effective Demand

Let's move on to Rueff's other two criticisms of the "General Theory." The first is that Keynesian theory assumes that prices and means of production are strictly blocked. Keynes himself did not mention the existence of such a precondition, however, Rueff cites specific passages showing Keynes's assumption of this. If such a precondition was assumed, he says, the solution to the unemployment problem should have included the option of "removing economic rigidities." Rueff implies that Keynes did not mention the preconditions because he did not want to admit that such a solution existed. This is evident in Keynes's wording in a letter he wrote to Rueff (May 20, 1932) saying that "*we must build* a device that can function without relying on flexibility" (emphasis added).

Rueff's remaining criticism is directed at the policy response to the unemployment problem suggested by Keynesian theory, namely, the creation of effective demand through public investment. According to Rueff, the only way the theory allows for the reduction of unemployment is to issue deficit-financed public bonds and carry out large-scale public investment. Such policies would lead to inflation and "general economic and social turmoil." If this policy continues indefinitely, we will finally have to limit individual freedom, and we will end up with "the economic system invented by Hitler." Thus, in the context of Rueff's critique of Keynes, Keynes was not an economist who revolutionized economics, but an economist who tried to help deprive people of their freedom. Or, to borrow a term from Rueff's scientific methodology, Keynesian theory is "Euclidean" only in a wartime economy where the movement of prices and means of production is blocked.

---

[3] AEF, B50525, Commissariat général du Plan, Groupe de travail. Monnaie, prix et croissance, séance du 11 avril 1972. Exposé de Jacques Rueff.

[4] In the 1970s when monetarism attracted attention, the central banks of the EEC member countries made researches on the relation between the volume of liquidity and inflation. These researches found a certain correlation between the two variables but concluded that the volume of liquidity could not be managed by policy measures. Nevertheless, the major central banks of Germany, France, and UK will set targets on monetary liquidity, expecting psychological effect of the targets.

The Tobin/Rueff Controversy

Tobin wrote a "comment" on Rueff's criticisms of General Theory in which he raises several questions (Tobin, 1948). Among them, the question directed at Rueff's third criticism is particularly interesting because such questions were shared not only by Tobin but also by other Keynesians and policymakers in various countries.

Tobin questions Rueff's characterization of deficit-financed government investment as a serious difficulty in Keynesian theory. According to Rueff, the only way to bring the economy out of recession through government investment is "a cruel dilemma of two choices": inflation or Hitler's regime. However, if investment, whether private or government, takes place, the asset stock of consumers and entrepreneurs will increase, and their propensity to consume will rise. The increase in assets will increase the cash stock of individuals, which is what Rueff focuses on. Moreover, in the first place, the average person cannot distinguish between "legitimate" dollars created by the free functioning of the market and "illegitimate" dollars derived from the issuance of deficit public debt.

These issues are addressed by Rueff as follows (Rueff, 1948). When the amount of currency created by the free market exceeds the market's needs, it is withdrawn from circulation as interest rates fall and prices rise. However, this adjustment mechanism does not work for currency created through the issuance of deficit-covered bonds, and inflation becomes inevitable. Therefore, economists, let alone the general public, must make a strict distinction between "legitimate" and "illegitimate" currencies.

Nevertheless, an increase in income due to increased employment will certainly increase the funds needed to repay the public debt. Rueff reinforces this point by stating that even if wealth equal to the amount of investment is produced, only a portion of this wealth will enter the national treasury. At the time, with the advent of Keynesian theory, optimism about deficit financing was spreading among policymakers, who believed that public finances should be balanced in the medium term. Rueff warned against this tendency.

As mentioned above, Rueff rejects the General Theory altogether. According to him, this theory applies only in special cases where the price mechanism and the movement of the means of production are blocked and the economy does not react at all to changes in prices and interest rates. Therefore, the General Theory does not deserve the name of "general theory."[5] Nevertheless, Keynesian theory as a remedy for unemployment has already been accepted in many countries, and it has "transcended the boundaries of economics to become a genuine instrument of governance" (Rueff, 1979, vol. II-2, pp. 272–273). Aware of this reality, Rueff concludes his article with the following apocalyptic prophecy.

> When the next recession comes, the policies proposed by Lord Keynes will be implemented worldwide. I assure you unhesitatingly – this policy will reduce unemployment only slightly, but it will have serious effects in the countries where it is implemented. The economic chaos that will result will reestablish throughout the world a system of general planning, akin to a wartime system, based on the total abolition of individual freedom.

---

[5] Rueff repeats this expression in his articles and in his autobiography.

> Perhaps because of Lord Keynes, the next cycle will be an opportunity for a major policy shift that some expect, and others fear. In any case, if measures are taken based on faulty theories, the results will be quite different from what is intended. If the measures are ineffective, the majority of the public will use them as a new basis for calling for the replacement of a regime that has betrayed and destroyed itself (Rueff, 1979, vol. II-2, pp. 300–301).

In recent years, empirical research on the post-World War II economic history of Western European countries has been progressing. In the light of the results of this research, Rueff's analysis has largely hit the nail on the head. Both the British and French governments tried to boost the economy during the downturn by public investment and monetary easing, and to sustain growth under a weak currency. This policy was effective in easing labor-management conflicts and maintaining social peace. However, it led to a widening budget deficit and balance of payments deficit, followed by currency instability, which eventually forced the governments to turn to a tightening policy. This was the so-called stop-and-go policy. When this policy came to a standstill, the government turned to the last resort of devaluing the currency. As I will show in detail later (in Chap. 12), after exhausting these usual policy measures by the end of the 1950s, France, under the authority of President Charles de Gaulle, implemented the neoliberal fiscal structural reform based on Rueff's proposal with great success. At any rate, Keynesian policies did not work as theorized in Western European countries (Gonjo, 2016).

6.2 The End of the Keynesian Era

In the 1970s, the Bretton Woods fixed exchange rate system collapsed, and the first oil crisis occurred on the heels of it. At that time, governments implemented Keynesian expansionary policies under the name of "economic stimulus," just as Rueff had predicted. However, this policy did not bring about economic recovery, but instead caused stagflation, where inflation and recession coexisted. Keynesian policies turned into a risk factor that destroyed the economy and society.

At the end of 1975, Rueff published his article, "The Age of Keynes," in the journal of the Paris Institute of Economic Research and in January 1976.[6] He presented the same paper at the annual meeting of the Mont Pèlerin Society in Paris. In addition, "The Age of Keynes" was re-titled "The End of the Keynesian Era" and reprinted in *Le Monde*, a high-class evening newspaper, and in *Euromoney*, an English-language magazine, in February and April 1976, respectively.

In "The End of the Keynesian Era," Rueff briefly refers to the contents of his own articles published in 1925, 1931, and 1947 and introduces two new arguments.

The first concerns the trends of the real wage rate and the unemployment rate in France during the period 1963–75 (inflationary period) which he shows in two

---

[6] Rueff, "L'ère keynésienne", Bulletin de l'Institut économique de Paris, novembre-décembre 1975, repris dans Rueff, 1979, vol. III-1. In the latter volume, the title of the article appears as "La fin de l'ère keynésienne" ("The end of Keynesian era").

curves (Fig. 6.3 in the article). The correlation between the two curves is similar to that of the United Kingdom in the 1920s (deflationary period). There is a disturbance in the correlation between September 1973 and September 1974, which is explained by the economic turmoil caused by the first oil crisis. He argues that his theory of unemployment, which ascribes the cause of unemployment to the rise in real wages, is a "general law" that can be confirmed regardless of the differences between countries and the different phases of economic change.

The second argument Rueff develops in the paper concerns the reasons why Keynesian theory has gained widespread support. Here, he focuses on two points. The first is that he, Keynes, focuses on the fact that workers are sensitive to a decline in nominal wages, not real wages, and makes this the basis of his theory. According to Rueff, Keynes derived this from his experience in the 1920s when wages did not fall in line with prices in Britain, which led to mass unemployment. Keynes subsequently came up with the idea to lower real wages in the roundabout way of raising general prices by increasing investment spending.

There is, however, another way to raise general prices, which is to increase consumption spending instead of investment spending. So why did Keynes choose investment spending instead of consumption spending? Rueff explains the reason as follows. Consumption spending is decided by individuals and is not at the disposal of

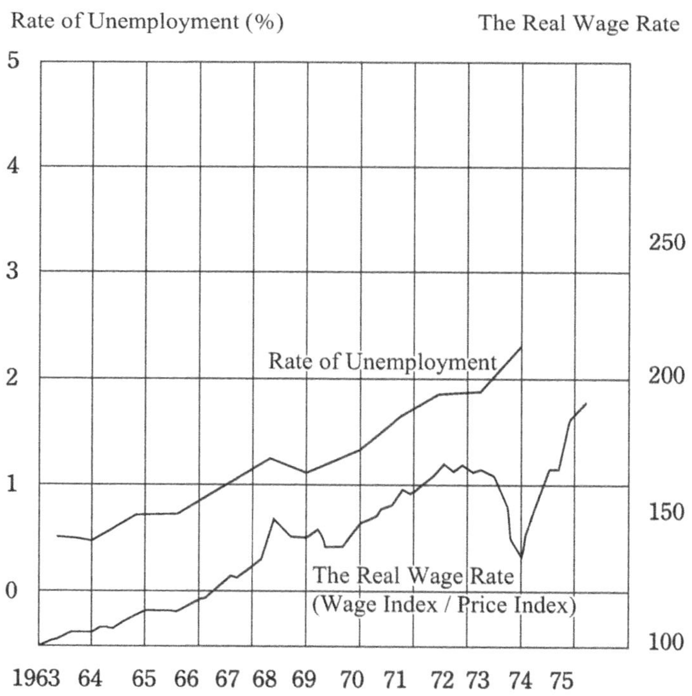

Fig. 6.3 Evolution of Unemployment in France (1963–1975). *Source* Rueff (1979, vol. III-1, p. 168)

the public authorities. Investment spending, on the other hand, is in the hands of the public authorities and can be implemented flexibly. Using this method, unemployment can be absorbed by generating inflation, and once unemployment is absorbed, sustained growth and excess employment can be guaranteed. The reason why countries set full employment as a policy goal after World War II was because they could count on the discretionary policy instrument of investment spending by public authorities.

Thus, Rueff concludes that the essence of Keynesian theory is to attract inflation through fiscal and monetary policies and to lower real wages "without tears." He calls this Keynes's "genius" and "the great secret of the Cambridge magician" (Rueff, 1979, vol. III-1, p. 174). According to Rueff, the difference between his and Keynes's response to the unemployment problem boils down to the difference in the method of adjusting the wage level to the general price level, that is, whether to achieve this by devaluing the currency (Rueff) or with the roundabout method of inflation (Keynes).

Yet western countries have been able to maintain full employment long after the war. Why is this so? The main reason, according to Rueff, is the global inflation that resulted from the excess of dollars under the Bretton Woods system. In other words, he says, this inflation adjusted real wages to the general price level.

At the end of his article, after confirming the situation current at the time (the mid-1970s) when countries were suffering from severe stagflation, Rueff quoted his own prophecy of 1947 verbatim. He died in 1978 and did not see the final fulfillment of his prophecy. Apart from the "reconstruction of the general planning system," it can be said that history unfolded according to his prophecy in two ways. First, in the 1970s, neoclassical economics emerged as the dominant economics in the West, replacing Keynesian theory. Then, in the late 1970s and early 1980s, Western European countries embarked on a long period of neoliberal structural reform (e.g., deregulation, privatization of state-owned enterprises) and began to make serious efforts to deepen European economic integration (especially monetary integration). Since the 1920s Rueff had been advocating the need to strengthen the functioning of market institutions and the need for economic integration in Europe, (the creation of a "Common Market"). The newly emerging world clearly overlapped with Rueff's vision (see Chap. 11). However, this was only the case until the 1990s when, with increasing globalization, softening, and servitization of the economy, a world quite different from that predicted by Rueff emerged.

Chapter 7
The Dollar and the International Monetary System After World War II—The Inherited Keynesian Approach

After regaining his freedom at the end of World War II, Rueff published his life's work, "Social Order," (1945), after which he became much more active as a lecturer and author. The topics he covered were diverse, but they can be roughly divided into two areas: the domestic economy and the international economy. The first area will be discussed in the last chapter of this book, and all the others will deal with the second area, especially the issue of the dollar and the reform of the international monetary system, a subject central to international discussions during the 1960s. Rueff's analysis of this situation and his theory of institutional reform, which advocates a return to the gold standard, were responsible for making his name widely known internationally.

In the end, Rueff's theory of reforming the international monetary system failed to move the entire international community. Nevertheless, his keen eyes for reality and uncompromising logic caused a huge stir among intellectuals. In the 1960s, he was invited to give a number of lectures in New York, Boston, and San Francisco, as well as in major European cities. His speeches were published one after another in leading newspapers and economic journals. In 1965, his speeches moved the French President Charles de Gaulle to the extent that, at a press conference in February of the same year, de Gaulle issued a statement fully in line with Rueff's arguments. Two months later, former U.S. Vice President Richard Nixon joined the audience at a congressional lecture Rueff gave in New York.

After de Gaulle's press conference, the international discussion on the dollar and the reform of the international monetary system shifted from a technical to a more political perspective. As a result, the relationship between Rueff's argument and reality also changed. In this chapter, I will deal with the period up to February 1960 and leave the later period to the next chapter.

Y. Gonjo et al., *The Truth of Liberal Economy*, Springer Studies in the History of Economic Thought, https://doi.org/10.1007/978-981-99-0841-7_7

7.1 The Dollar Gap and Inflation

As a member of the United Nations Committee on Economic and Employment Affairs, Rueff was an early voice, yet a critical one, on the postwar international monetary system and currency issues. His first serious paper in this area, on the so-called dollar gap, the shortage of the dollar as a settlement currency in European countries, was published from March to April 1949 (Rueff, 1949/1979, vol. III-2). At about the same time, he gave lectures in Paris, Brussels, Rome, and Zurich, where he also addressed this issue.

Rueff's views on the balance of payments remained unchanged since the transfer dispute with Keynes in 1949. He continued with the classical theory that, quite simply, the balance of payments is automatically balanced, thus, if this theory is applied, there can be no long-term shortage of foreign currency for international payments. However, after World War II, the latter situation became the norm in European countries. Rueff's article in 1949 attempts to explain this anomaly.

His paper begins with theory which is followed, as usual, by factual verification. Theories of the balance of payments refined by economists since Robert Torrens and David Ricardo, all agree that the balance of payments tends to balance automatically and Rueff first confirms this.

In previous debates with Keynes, Rueff had cited the French case exclusively for purposes of factual verification. This time, however, he also cites the case of Germany from the stabilization of the mark until 1931 when exchange controls were introduced. In both France and Germany, until the collapse of the world economy and the plunge into the bloc economy, the balance of payments was maintained by flexible expansion and contraction of the trade balance when there was a large inflow of capital from abroad or compensation payments to foreign countries, or when these payments stopped. This, Rueff argues, confirms the correctness of the classical theory of the balance of payments.

So why do European countries continue to experience balance of payments imbalances and dollar shortages despite the guaranteed convertibility of their currencies under the IMF regime? Rueff believes it is because there has been a major change in the environment in which the balance of payments adjustment mechanism operates. The three changes are inflation, the unfreezing of funds in return for Marshall aid, and circumstances related to the operation of the IMF. In the postwar period, European countries recorded large budget deficits due to the implementation of reconstruction projects, and their economies suffered from inflation. Inflation caused by these budget deficits is the main cause of the dollar gap. Rueff explains his rationale in the following terms.

The state of the balance of payments from time to time affects, first, the total amount of domestic purchasing power obtained through the sale of wealth supplied to the market, and second, through this total purchasing power, the level of domestic prices and interest rates. It also adjusts the balance of payments through the convertibility of the currency with gold or foreign currencies, leading it to equilibrium. Therefore, when the balance of foreign debt is cleared, the domestic purchasing power is reduced by that amount. As a result, there will be a shortage of purchasing power available to purchase the products supplied to the market at market prices. The shortage of purchasing power thus created causes prices and interest rates to fluctuate, leading to an equilibrium in the balance of payments.

As it happens, if a nation is unable to raise the necessary financial resources through taxes and government bonds, it has no choice but to issue new currency. If new purchasing power is created in this way, the reduction in purchasing power resulting from the liquidation of external debt will be reduced by the amount of purchasing power created. If the amount of purchasing power created exceeds the balance of payments deficit, the effect of the deficit on the reduction of purchasing power will be canceled out, and the balance of payments deficit will increase. Thus, fiscal inflation distorts the automatic adjustment mechanism of the balance of payments and prolongs the state of imbalance in the balance of payments.

The above is a phenomenon that occurs between a country with fiscal inflation and a country with zero inflation, but the same thing also occurs between countries with different inflation rates. For example, the inflation rate in the United States is lower than that of European countries. If international trade was directed by changes in relative prices resulting from changes in aggregate purchasing power, all trading partners would have a deficit with respect to the United States. This is the true nature of the dollar gap. As with the relationship between the U.S. and European countries, there are differences in inflation rates among European countries as well, which creates a shortage of settlement currencies. This is why the dollar gap problem is so widespread.

Thus, the only way to close the dollar gap is to revive the balance of payments adjustment mechanism by ending inflation. However, policymakers and economists in many countries were reluctant to accept this solution. Rueff later explained why. Like Keynes in the German transfer controversy, most of them believed that international trade was determined by the structural factors of each country and the intervention of the government to correct them, and that it could not be changed by monetary or fiscal policy (Rueff, 1977, p. 271).

7.2 Restoration of Currency Convertibility and the Gold Exchange Standard

Postwar reconstruction is almost complete by the mid-1950s. Inflation begins to end in most countries, the shortage of dollars is almost over, and momentum is building for the restoration of currency convertibility. Rueff begins to act in anticipation of these changes. He realizes that if the currencies of each country are restored to convertibility, the risks lurking in the postwar international monetary system, namely, the gold exchange standard with the dollar as the reserve currency, will become apparent, and the restructuring of the international monetary system will surely be addressed in international discussions.

In the early 1930s, Rueff had already examined the Great Recession of 1931–34 in detail from a monetary perspective and concluded that the gold exchange standard was the main cause of the Great Recession (see Chap. 5, Sect. 5.3). This view was carefully developed into a theory in relation to the dollar problem after the end of the 1950s. His original theories on the gold exchange standard theoretically informed his criticism of the international monetary system and his theory of its reform in the 1960s. Let us begin with a review of Rueff's theory of the gold exchange standard, based on the article he wrote for *Le Monde* at the end of June 1961 (Rueff, 1961/1980, vol. III-2).

7.2.1 An "Inherently Inflationary" Gold Exchange Standard

To make it easier to understand, let's take the example of a bilateral relationship between the United States, the reserve currency nation, and France, which holds dollars as reserves.

If the U.S. balance of payments deficit is caused by importing goods from France or extending credit to France, this deficit will be settled in dollars. The dollars transferred to France through the settlement are recorded as deposits on the balance sheet of the local bank. These deposits are then lent out to individuals and companies, which in turn issue currency (deposit currency). Moreover, the issuance of currency is multiplicative. The dollars are eventually bought up by the central bank (Banque de France) and transferred to its reserves. Since the central bank has no domestic source for the dollars it buys up, it immediately sends the foreign currency to New York and deposits it in local banks to earn money. The dollars returned to New York, the source of the transfer, in the form of French credits, are the so-called dollar balance. The banks in New York, like the banks in France, will lend their deposits to individuals and businesses, and in doing so, they will issue currency in multiples.

In the above scenario under the gold exchange standard, both the United States and France would increase their currencies, which led Rueff to characterize this international monetary system as "essentially inflationary" (Rueff, 1980, vol. III-2, p. 103).

Under a gold standard, balance of payments deficits would be settled in gold, and the amount of currency in circulation in the United States, a country with a balance of payments deficit, would shrink. As a result, the purchasing power of the country will decrease, and the balance of payments will automatically adjust to restore equilibrium. Under the gold exchange standard, however, even if the U.S. balance of payments runs into the red and dollars flow out, the amount of currency in circulation in the United States does not shrink because the outflow returns to the source like a boomerang. Thus, theoretically, the reserve currency nation could accumulate foreign credit indefinitely without worrying about balance of payments deficits, and the countries that accepted the credit could continue to borrow without worrying about repayment. In other words, "lending and borrowing without tears" can be repeated.

At first glance, the relationship between the U.S. balance of payments deficit and the dollar balance resembles that of a chicken and an egg. In fact, it may be said that the increase in the dollar balance was the result of the U.S. balance of payments deficit. However, according to Rueff, this is not true, because "the increase in the dollar balance is the cause, and the balance of payments deficit is the result" (Rueff, 1965, p. 35). He also argues that the fact that the balance of payments deficit is maintained at the level of the dollar balance—that is, the fact that the balance of payments "imbalance" becomes the norm—does not mean that there is a mechanism that guarantees balance of payments equilibrium through the transfer of purchasing power. The fact that balance of payments "imbalances" becomes the norm—is quantitative proof of the existence of a mechanism that guarantees balance of payments equilibrium through the transfer of purchasing power, and that this mechanism is sensitive and powerful (Rueff, 1965, p. 35). In short, Rueff argues that Keynes and his followers who reject the classical theory are wrong, and he describes the current gold exchange standard "as the most ridiculous payment system imaginable" (Rueff, 1965/1980, vol. III-2, p. 188).

According to Rueff, under the gold exchange standard, when large-scale international capital movements occur, there is a massive increase in currency which leads to higher prices and an exchange boom. The global boom on the eve of the Great Depression was just such an event, and it was the monetary factor that triggered the Great Recession of 1931–34. As we will see in more detail in a later section, Rueff warns that the Western world since the end of the 1950s is in danger of reaching a similar situation.

I would like to add one more point about the gold exchange standard. Rueff believes that the post-World War II international monetary system is riddled with serious contradictions, and that the system will eventually become unsustainable. In this respect, his view resembles that of a theory known as the "liquidity dilemma" made known by Robert Triffin in a paper he published in 1959 (Triffin, 1960). Rueff, however, had been concerned with the flaws of the gold exchange standard long before his *Le Monde* article in 1961. For this reason, the "liquidity dilemma" is sometimes referred to as the "Rueff-Triffin dilemma" in European countries, especially in the French-speaking world. There is, however, an essential difference between Triffin and Rueff in terms of theory. Triffin sees that under the postwar international monetary system, the supply of dollars will not be able to keep up with the growing demand for international liquidity. Rueff, on the other hand, believes that under this monetary system, the world economy will fall into inflation. It is thus problematic to lump the two dilemmas together.

Nevertheless, the international monetary system after World War II was rebuilt as the gold exchange standard without sufficient discussion, despite the abhorrent experience of the 1930s. The reconstructed international monetary system, like the old system, is inflationary and has the potential to cause a serious crisis. This was Rueff's basic perception of the international monetary system after World War II.

7.2.2 *Restoration of Currency Convertibility and the Issue of International Monetary System Reform*

At the end of December 1958, European countries simultaneously restored the convertibility of their currencies. This triggered a massive influx of short-term capital from the United States into Germany and France, causing stock prices in both countries to soar. A phenomenon similar to that on the eve of the Great Depression appeared and if left unchecked, a "new Great Depression" may have occurred.

Several alternatives to the gold exchange standard were already known, including the Keynesian and Triffin proposals. However, according to Rueff, all of them had their problems, and action at the government level was urgently needed to prevent a new Great Depression. In June 1959, he sent a memorandum to Antoine Pinay, Minister of Finance, suggesting that a subcommittee be set up within the French government to begin the process of establishing an international mechanism for bailing out the dollar. Rueff apparently hoped that Pinay would appoint him as the head of this subcommittee. Pinay, however, brushed aside Rueff's suggestion owing to the following reason. The majority of senior officials in the French finance ministry and central bank after World War II, like their colleagues in other countries, were opposed to the idea of restoring free markets with a functioning price mechanism. For this reason, they regarded Rueff as a heretic and were extremely reluctant to have him involved with government agencies.

During this period, a large amount of gold flowed out of the United States in conjunction with the outflow of short-term capital, and conversely, the central banks of European countries all increased their gold reserves substantially. Confidence in the dollar declined, and in October 1960, the price of an ounce of gold on the London free gold market rose to a high of $40, well above the official price of $35. The following November, a gold pool system was organized to stabilize the gold price. In the United States, President Dwight D. Eisenhower, who was nearing the end of his term, issued an emergency directive to improve the international balance of payments. The following year, on February 6, 1961, John F. Kennedy, who had just been inaugurated as President, frankly admitted in a special letter to Congress (giving specific figures) that the dollar was in a worrisome situation.

The new President Kennedy was to visit France from the end of May to the beginning of June 1961. Prior to that, on March 16 of the same year, Rueff met with de Gaulle. Just before the meeting, Rueff stayed in Washington for 3 days to exchange views on international monetary issues with his old acquaintance William McChesney Martin, Chairman of the Board of Governors of the Federal Reserve System, and two Assistant Secretaries of the Treasury, one of whom was Robert V. Roosa, also an old acquaintance. Rueff explained to de Gaulle the latest situation regarding the dollar and the international monetary system and said that the system threatened to bring a serious crisis to the Western world, and hoped that de Gaulle would intervene. Let me quote the concluding part of his speech.

> The Federal Reserve would fail tomorrow if the Western issuing banks exercised their right to their listed and short-term deposits [i.e., dollar balances] in the New York market. Of

course, these banks would not do that unless they were under a political or financial threat. Nevertheless, in the face of such a threat, they will be forced to put their own currency first, rather than the dollar, as they did in 1956. A virtual suspension of payments in the U.S. monetary system would put the entire West in grave danger (cited in Rueff, 1977, vol. I, p. 262).

At that time, Rueff told de Gaulle about the Kennedy administration's lack of interest in the dollar crisis, information which he had obtained from the three heads of the U.S. monetary and financial authorities to the effect that Kennedy does not remember what he said in the Presidential Special Teachings, and no one reminded him of the contents of the Teachings. The three men in charge, among them the Chairman of the Federal Reserve, believed that the dollar crisis could be solved in less than a year by curbing foreign payments. When Rueff explained to them the serious problems of the current international monetary system, all three "seemed moved and astonished to admit that they had no objection to [Rueff's] arguments and to the conclusions that could be drawn from them" (Rueff, 1977, vol. I, p. 261).

Later, at the end of June, Rueff wrote an article in *Le Monde* with the same contents as his explanation to de Gaulle (Rueff, 1961/1980, vol. III-2). This article was immediately reprinted in *The Times* and *Fortune*, the leading newspapers and magazines in Britain and the United States, as well as in Germany, Italy, and the West, as a whole. The Western media's strong interest in Rueff's article shows that his argument belonged to unchartered territory in the eyes of the international community.

At this time, Rueff frequently met with de Gaulle and his staff in the presidential office to advise them on international monetary issues. In this way, the French presidency was occupied by supporters of Rueff's theory, led by the chief cabinet secretary Etienne Burin des Roziers, unlike the Ministry of Finance and the Central Bank.

7.3 The Gold Exchange Standard and the Dollar Problem

Immediately after Kennedy's Special Teachings in February, 1961, the finance ministries and central bankers of the United States and major Western countries began discussions on how to deal with the dollar crisis and how to strengthen the functions of the IMF. Two results of these discussions in 1962 were the issuance of Roosa Bonds and the conclusion of a swap agreement between the Bank of France, 10 other major central banks, and the Bank for International Settlements and the U.S. Federal Reserve System. Roosa of the U.S. Treasury Department played a central role in the discussions.

In the summer of 1963, the policy of the U.S. government was solidified. First, on July 18 of the same year, Kennedy announced a plan to improve the international balance of payments in a special letter. Like Eisenhower's emergency directive, the plan was aimed at reducing foreign payments and increasing foreign payments to the United States. Instead, the document postponed a fundamental reform of the international monetary system as a task to be tackled after the U.S. balance of payments was restored to balance. In short, the views that Rueff had shared with U.S. financial and monetary officials were not ultimately reflected in the policies of the U.S. government.

Then, in October of the same year, Roosa published an article titled "International Monetary System Reform" in *Foreign Affairs* magazine, in which he made public his in-depth views on international monetary system reform. The IMF, the OECD (Organization for Economic Co-operation and Development) and the G10 had begun talks on international monetary reform in 1962, and Roosa's views had set the tone for these talks. This motivated Rueff's confrontation.

7.3.1 How to Prepare for an International Liquidity Shortage—Roosa's View

In the op-ed for *Foreign Affairs* (Roosa, 1967), Roosa considers three options for reforming the international monetary system, the first of which is to adopt the gold standard, and the second, to introduce a floating exchange rate. Both have major drawbacks which make them untenable, according to Roosa.[1]

First of all, since World War I and especially since World War II, governments have played a much larger role in the economic sphere, and international economic relations have become much more complex. Therefore, it is unrealistic to adopt a gold standard that leaves the coordination to the market mechanism. A floating exchange rate system, on the other hand, is also unrealistic because it impedes trade and international capital flows. Significantly Roosa gives priority to short-term political or practical circumstances, not to theory.

The third option, which Roosa supports, is to maintain the IMF system, or the gold exchange standard. However, he says that the current system needs reinforcement to be able to meet the real needs of the world and he devotes a lot of attention to the details of such reinforcement. His strategy at the time can be summarized as follows.

The key to reforming the international monetary system is to take steps to ensure the stability and flexibility of liquidity needed for growth in the West as a whole (including developing countries) over the medium to long term. To do this, Roosa says, we need to "include more resilient and larger foreign exchange or international credit in our reserves." He is particularly concerned about the shortage of international liquidity expected when the United States achieves a return to balance of payments. Roosa argues for the need to prepare for this in advance. However, he is optimistic that "through a gradual process of reform, we will be able to reach our goal," since the talks among major countries have already produced satisfactory results and President Kennedy has expressed his determination to make serious efforts to restore balance of payments.

---

[1] Roosa's view had been precisely developed in his work published a year later his retirement from Assistant Secretary of the Treasury (Roosa, 1965). His view brilliantly followed the U.S. national interest.

In short, it is possible to secure the international liquidity necessary for the growth of Western countries through "gradual reforms" in cooperation with other major countries, and there is no need for a drastic reform of the international monetary system. This was the core of Roosa's view. His concept of reforming the international monetary system was based on the idea of managing credit internationally and can be seen as an expansion of the Keynesian theory of domestic credit management into the international sphere. This is akin to the "locomotive theory" that developed at the OECD in the late 1970s and is a kind of "international Keynesianism" (Gayon, 2017).

7.3.2 *The Problem is not a "Liquidity Problem" but a "Coordination Problem"—Rueff's View*

Following the successive clarification of his position by the U.S. President and the U.S. officials, Rueff delivered a public lecture in November 1963 in which he made a full-scale criticism of the U.S. government's stance from both theoretical and empirical perspectives. The manuscript of this lecture, with some additions, was included in his book "The Troublesome Problem of Balance of Payments" (Rueff, 1965). It was the most systematic of his many lectures and articles on the dollar and the international monetary system.

At the beginning of the lecture, Rueff summarizes the issues surrounding the dollar crisis and the international monetary system as follows. The U.S. government's view is that it can balance its balance of payments without reforming the international monetary system, which is the same as Keynes's view in the German transfer debate where Keynes argued that Germany's reparations payments must be adjusted to an amount that is transferable to Germany, i.e., the balance of payments. According to Keynes, the various elements of the balance of payments, especially the balance of trade, are determined by structural factors specific to the trading parties and are not affected by changes in income, prices, or exchange rates. So Kennedy's Special Teachings, which sought to mobilize administrative means to bring foreign payments in line with the country's own solvency, was a typically Keynesian approach.

Faced with a sharp decline in foreign exchange reserves in 1957, the French government took the same approach as the U.S. government and tried to respond in the same way. It introduced a strong protectionist trade policy in the form of import quotas to bring its foreign payments in line with its own solvency. However, this policy failed, and the decline in foreign exchange reserves did not stop. In the final stage of the crisis, the French government, having run out of options, adopted a plan for fiscal structural reform proposed by a government committee headed by Rueff, and escaped the crisis by restoring the free functioning of the market. This was called the "miracle" of France.

Having experienced such success in his own country, Rueff questions the policy choices of the U.S. government. Shouldn't the United States adopt the opposite policy? In other words, "Isn't the current deficit in the U.S. balance of payments due to a dysfunctional price mechanism, rather than to rigidities in the main items [of the balance of payments]?" If that is the case, then the answer is to rebuild an effective mechanism for international payments, not to manipulate it arbitrarily (Rueff, 1965).

Next, Rueff verifies that his judgment is correct from both theoretical and empirical perspectives. This part of the paper is basically the same as the 1949 paper dealing with the dollar gap. The difference is that the U.S. balance of payments after World War II is the subject of the verification. Rueff pays particular attention to the following two facts in the U.S. balance of payments. First, on the one hand, the massive foreign military expenditures, foreign aid, and corporate foreign direct investment transactions that do not appear in customs statistics, have resulted in a huge deficit in the balance of payments, while on the other hand, the trade balance has recorded an unprecedentedly large surplus. Secondly, the surplus in the balance of trade fluctuated in the same direction and on the same scale as the transactions not shown in the customs statistics. According to Rueff, neither the huge trade balance surplus nor the fluctuations in this surplus should be seen as coincidental. It is the result of a myriad of economic actions taken by government agencies, individuals and private companies based on their own judgment, sensitive to changes in prices, interest rates and exchange rates. In other words, it is the work of the "invisible hand."

In short, according to Rueff, the automatic adjustment mechanism of the balance of payments works strictly in the United States as well as in France and Germany. If the U.S. government cuts military spending or foreign aid, the trade surplus will fall in tandem, leaving the balance of payments deficit untouched. In a lecture he gave in New York in April 1965, these issues were put in simple terms:

> There are those who believe that balance of payments deficits can be corrected by reducing foreign payments, such as military spending, foreign aid, or exchange controls. But this is just a false hope. As you can see from what I have said above, cutting those foreign payments would reduce the very high U.S. trade surplus. However, this will not affect the balance of payments. Therefore, the U.S. balance of payments deficit will continue as long as the [current] international monetary system remains in place.[2]

So why has the U.S. balance of payments deficit become so entrenched that it threatens the credibility of the dollar? Rueff analyzes the reasons. It was not until 1958 that the previous dollar shortage turned into a dollar surplus. During this period, there were no structural changes in either the United States or European countries. Therefore, the excess of dollars must be viewed as a phenomenon originating from the following mechanism of the gold exchange standard. With the restoration of currency convertibility in European countries, short-term capital flowed out of the United States to these countries, creating a huge dollar balance, or short-term debt for the United States. The important point here is that the cause is the increase in the dollar balance, and the difference between the trade balance surplus and the transactions that do not show up in tariff statistics—that is, the factors that prevent

[2] *Broadening the Dimensions of Publics Affairs*, National Industrial Conference Report, N3, New York, 1965.

the balance of payments from being balanced—is the result of the increase in the dollar balance.

From the above, Rueff draws two "political conclusions." The first is that the United States cannot be expected to reduce its foreign payments. The only way to restore confidence in the dollar is to replace the current international monetary system with a gold standard. The second issue concerns how to stop the outflow of gold. The Federal Reserve currently sets the interest rate at which it intervenes in the open market below the level of money market rates. Raising this rate would stop the outflow of gold. In short, the "political conclusion" of Rueff was to transform the system and monetary policy so that the price mechanism could function fully. This means that the problem is not a "liquidity problem" or a "structural problem" but a "coordination problem" in relation to the "lack of liquidity" that Roosa had raised in his article of October 1963 (Rueff, 1965/1980, vol. III-2, p. 103).

When Rueff included the above speech from 1963 in his book in 1965, he refused to consider the recent increase in Euro-dollars in the speech. He did mention the Euro-dollar in connection with the dollar crisis several times in his later papers. In the end, however, he sees it, like swap agreements and SDRs (special drawing rights), as a liquidity resource designed to make up for the shortfall in gold caused by the unreasonably low valuation of the gold price.[3]

[3] "Introduction to the Japanese Edition", translation of (Rueff, 1971).

Chapter 8
The Dollar and the International Monetary System After World War II—Rueff's Struggle

After Kennedy's Special Teachings to the U.S. Congress in 1961, talks began among the major countries about saving the dollar and reinforcing the international monetary system. Some of the results, such as the conclusion of swap agreements and the issuance of Roosa Bonds, were implemented during 1962. On the other hand, the IMF, OECD, and G10 expert committees continued to discuss various institutional measures, such as the creation of international reserve assets and the capital increase of the IMF. All of the measures discussed were in line with the principles set forth in the Kennedy Special Teachings on Balance of Payments and the Roosa Paper of 1963. The first principle was to give priority to restoring balance of payments in the United States. The second principle was to leave the reform of the international monetary system itself as a future task and to meet the demand for international liquidity through "gradual reform" of the system for the time being.

In short, the response to the dollar and international monetary system problem was probably limited to technical aspects at first. However, the situation changed drastically when de Gaulle spoke about this issue at a press conference on February 4, 1960. Thereafter, the issue became a political one.

8.1 Press Conference by President de Gaulle

At this press conference, de Gaulle expressed his views on the international monetary system in response to questions from journalists (I will refer to his views as "statement"). In the fall of the previous year, the pound sterling crisis broke out, and at the same time, the dollar was being sold in large quantities. The United Kingdom asked the IMF for $100 million, and the United States dealt with the crisis by issuing Roosa Bonds and withdrawing several hundred million dollars by swap operations. De Gaulle witnessed the crisis held a press conference.

The de Gaulle statement can be divided into two major parts. The first half is devoted to the history of the gold exchange standard and its current status. This part

Y. Gonjo et al., *The Truth of Liberal Economy*, Springer Studies in the History of Economic Thought, https://doi.org/10.1007/978-981-99-0841-7_8

was based on Rueff's explanation to de Gaulle in 1961, which Rueff subsequently summarized in an article that was published throughout Western countries. In addition, the seriousness of the situation since then is further addressed. The total amount of gold reserves held by the central banks of European countries is now approaching the size of the gold reserves of the U.S. Federal Reserve System. The current international monetary system is not only at odds with reality but also threatens to plunge the Western world into a catastrophe in the near future.

The second half of the statement consists of a political assessment of the international monetary system and proposals for its fundamental reform and is also based on Rueff's article. The main points are as follows. Under the current system, only the United States (and to a lesser extent the United Kingdom) borrows money from the rest of the world free of charge under the so-called reserve currency privilege, and so the world is asymmetrical in terms of currency. International trade must be conducted on the basis of a currency that is impeccable in terms of materials and "without the stamp of any nation," as it was before World War I. Since there is no such currency other than gold, it is desirable to restore the gold standard. This would require transitional measures, which could be considered by the IMF, the G10, and the European Economic Community (EEC).

The statement concluded with the words, "France stands ready to participate actively in the major reforms that will be needed in the future for the benefit of the entire world" (De Gaulle, 1970, pp. 330–334)

In this way, de Gaulle's statement can be said to have given a political angle to Rueff's theory. The main point of de Gaulle's strategy was to weaken the power of both the United States and the United Kingdom. So that France could exercise its influence in the international arena on equal terms with both countries. If the gold standard was restored, the world would become symmetrical in terms of currencies, and both Britain and the United States would lose the reserve currency privileges they had enjoyed under the gold exchange standard. There was an excellent affinity between Rueff's argument and de Gaulle's strategy.

One week after the press conference, Valéry Giscard d'Estaing, Minister of Finance, made a speech on France's international monetary policy to complement de Gaulle's statement. At the IMF Annual Meetings, Giscard d'Estaing declared his opposition to the gold exchange standard but urged that "credit instruments" other than gold be added to the international liquidity to meet future liquidity shortages. (In February 1960, however, the U.S. government announced its firm intention to introduce a gold exchange standard.) In his February 1960 speech, Giscard d'Estaing called on countries to make international payments only in gold and to gradually reduce their reserve currency holdings of dollars, stating that France would henceforth base its monetary policy on the principle of the gold standard.

Giscard d'Estaing's speech in itself was not new. Since the restoration of currency convertibility at the end of 1958, Western European countries such as France, the Netherlands, and Switzerland had basically implemented monetary policies based on the principles of the gold standard, with the exception of West Germany, a divided country where, under pressure from the United States, the dollar could not be freely exchanged for gold. The significance of this speech lies in the fact that it openly called for other countries to follow France's example (Institut Charles de Gaulle, 1992, p. 150).

Understandably the United States was directly affected by de Gaulle's press conference and the press conference was generally perceived as "anti-American." De Gaulle himself expected such a reaction, and chose his words carefully in his statement in consideration for the United States. Nevertheless, if the United States loses its reserve currency privileges by restoring the gold standard, the country's influence in international politics will also decline so de Gaulle's press conference was not a pleasant one for the American people.

The reaction of the American public aside, it is important to note how the American officials analyzed this conference thereafter. In 1990, Robert Solomon made an interesting point speaking at a research conference in Paris to commemorate the 100th anniversary of de Gaulle's birth. Solomon was an economist from the U.S. Federal Reserve System and was deeply involved in the issue of international monetary system reform in the 1960s, including serving as the U.S. representative to the Third Committee of the OECD and witnessing the establishment of the SDR in the Expert Committee of the G10.

Solomon praised the French President's recognition of this problem area, at the time, and de Gaulle's evident familiarity with the history of the international monetary system as well as its technical aspects. He then indicates two important discrepancies that existed between President de Gaulle's approach at that press conference, on the one hand, and the claims and proposals made to international organizations by the representatives of French economic and financial authorities represented by Giscard d'Estaing, on the other. First, since 1963, French representatives had proposed the creation of an international reserve currency called "Collective Reserve Unit" (CRU) in the G-10 technical committee, which de Gaulle had not mentioned. Secondly, as shown by Giscard d'Estaing's statement at the IMF Annual Meeting in Tokyo, French economic and financial authorities adhered to the framework of the discussion prepared by the U.S. government as well as representatives of the United States and other countries until the autumn of 1964. De Gaulle, however, had insisted only on the necessity of returning to the gold standard (Institut Charles de Gaulle, 1992, p. 127).

That Solomon paid attention to these two points suggests that the U.S. officials recognized that France had broken away from its traditional policy of international cooperation and rejected the "gradual" reform of the international monetary system. After de Gaulle's press conference, the United States became firmer in its stance on the international monetary system and took a confrontational stance toward France.

8.2 The Idea of Raising the Gold Price Rejected by the Superpowers

Once the president of his own country issued a statement that was in line with Rueff's long-standing claims, Rueff no longer needed to be constrained in what he said. From this point on, Rueff responded to requests for speeches from various countries and began to speak actively about a specific or what he called a "constructive" reform plan for the international monetary system. He chose the lectures in New York and London on April 15 and May 24–25, 1960, respectively, as the first occasions to present this reform plan to the public in a coherent form (Rueff, 1980, vol. III-2, pp. 180–195). Rueff's New York lecture was held in the context of the Congressional Hearings. The following is a summary of his vision at this time.

The current state of the international monetary system closely resembles that of the Great Recession of 1931–33. The measures taken by the U.S. government so far to deal with the balance of payments deficit and the dollar crisis have all been in the realm of stalling. The balance of payments deficit is increasing by $2 billion annually, while gold reserves are decreasing by $10 billion. If this trend continues, we will undoubtedly face a serious crisis. The crisis is not limited to the United States. It is a "crisis of Western Europe" and a "crisis of civilization."

The only way to avoid a crisis is to resume international settlement in gold. However, in that case, the United States would be forced to liquidate its massive foreign debt, and the United States currently does not have the money necessary to do so. However, according to Rueff, there are ways to make the liquidation possible. One is Robert Triffin's idea of giving an international monetary organization like the IMF the power to issue a new international currency. The downside to this idea is that it could open the door to inflation. The second is Rueff's own proposal to double the price of gold in dollars and pay off the debt with the resulting increase in the nominal value of the gold stock. The reason for doubling the gold price is that prices in the United States have doubled since President Franklin Roosevelt devalued the dollar from $20.67 to $35 per ounce of gold in February 1934. Doubling the price of gold would leave the United States with $300 billion in gold holdings. Since the total U.S. debt to the central banks of other countries is $130 billion, there would still be $170 billion left after paying off the debt. In this way, the U.S. economy will not fall into deflation.

Rueff's proposal was supported by the following idea: the lack of liquidity is not a problem because of a lack of gold weight. The problem is not a shortage of gold weight, but a shortage of the nominal price of gold, because the price of gold is fixed at a low level, despite the fact that prices have risen dramatically. Raising the price of gold to match the current price level would solve the problem and increase the amount of gold mined. Thanks to the devaluation of the dollar in February 1934, Western civilization was able to escape the danger of collapse. America needs to do the same again, says Rueff.

Like the United States, the other reserve currency nation, the United Kingdom, needs to liquidate its pound balance. However, the situation is somewhat different from that of the dollar. The U.K.'s debt is to the former Dominion countries, and there is a gentlemen's agreement between the former Dominion countries and the United Kingdom. A scheme similar to that of the dollar can be applied to the liquidation of this pound balance. Nevertheless, because of the small amount of gold held by Britain, the pound balance cannot be liquidated even by doubling the price of gold. However, it is possible to liquidate the balance by adopting the method of international financial support for the United Kingdom.

Rueff's proposal here to raise the price of gold is similar to the devaluation of the dollar. The devaluation of a currency is a taboo subject in any country, and Rueff knew that the United States was no exception. For this reason, he stressed the major differences between his vision and the devaluation of the dollar in February 1934. First, the gold price would be raised before, not after, the crisis (as it was after the Great Depression). Second, other Western countries should sign international agreements to raise the gold price at the same time and in the same proportion as the United States. If this is done, it need not be called devaluation of the dollar. Of course, if countries other than the United States and United Kingdom raise the price of gold, inflation will occur in those countries. However, inflation could be avoided by lending half of the nominal increase in gold reserves resulting from the revaluation of gold to the United Kingdom to help clear the pound balance and using the other half to pay off the debt to the central bank of the country. The grandiose nature of Rueff's vision raised the question of its feasibility, but he himself believed that if the United States agreed, other countries would follow suit.

The audience's reaction to his speech in New York in April 1965 was said to be positive, and Rueff was applauded. However, he was then told by the Chairman of the Board of Governors of the Federal Reserve System that three of the five Federal Reserve governors on the Federal Open Market Committee were opposed to a change in the gold price. Therefore, "our position is set, and it cannot be changed." Upon hearing this, Rueff warned the Chairman, "If that is the case, the U.S. should not prevent countries with dollar balances from demanding the exchange of dollars for gold. However, the U.S. will be forced to suspend gold payments if it accedes to this demand" (Rueff, 1965/1967, pp. 510–511).

While proposing an increase in the price of gold, Rueff also sharply criticized the efforts being made by international organizations to increase international liquidity. In September 1965, just before the annual meeting of the IMF, he wrote an article for *Le Monde* and *The Times* entitled "Irrigation Planning in the Midst of Flooding" (Rueff, 1965/1980, vol. III-2), in which he harshly criticized the members of the G10 expert committee (chaired at the time by Rinaldo Ossola). His main criticisms can be summed up as follows.

In countries other than the United States and the United Kingdom, there is an excess of currency. These countries are experiencing inflation and have "stability plans" and "income policies" in place. There is no shortage of liquidity in the world as a whole; only the two reserve currency countries, the United States and the United Kingdom, have a need for international payment instruments. Only these two countries need currencies other than the dollar and the pound to cover their balance of payments deficits without losing or borrowing new money. The financial experts sent by countries to the IMF and the G10 are "watering the fields amid a flood" or "studying how to cope with a possible future drought while the rains continue to fall." They are the "naked kings" of Andersen's fairy tales. The responsibility of the G10 is particularly grave. They are trying to create liquidity in the name of the "general interest," as if all Western countries were parties, when only the United States and the United Kingdom are interested parties. If we continue in this manner, we will eventually have a "serious problem." What is needed is not a bailout of the dollar through international cooperation, but an "effective reform of the international monetary system."

8.3 The United States on the Offensive, The Isolation of France and Rueff, and the Growing Dollar Crisis

8.3.1 Turning the Tables and Isolating France

Pierre Esteva, Deputy Director of International Economies at the French Ministry of Finance in 1965, testified that from the middle of that year, the United States became even more adamant about its traditional position (Institut Charles de Gaulle, 1992, pp. 150–151). In fact, in July of the same year, Henry H. Fowler, who had just assumed the post of Secretary of the Treasury, announced a plan to improve the soundness of the balance of payments and clearly stated that the U.S. balance of payments deficit would be eliminated by the end of 1966. In line with this, the EEC countries also began to distance themselves from France. The fact that France was becoming more isolated in the EEC after de Gaulle came back to power made it difficult for Western European countries to sympathize with France (Gonjo, 2013, pp. 32–36).

Furthermore, the attitude of the economic and financial bureaucrats in each country was also problematic. They were of the postwar generation and had been baptized in Keynesianism and knew nothing about policies other than intervention by administrative means. That is why they feared that a return to the gold standard and a revival of the price mechanism could lead to unforeseen problems. It was not until the 1980s that the bureaucrats of European countries (with the exception of West Germany) broke free from the spell of interventionism that had taken hold through the two world wars (Gonjo, 2020). Therefore, their negative reaction in the 1960s is understandable.

At any rate, the EEC countries as well as the United States and Britain did not respond positively to the calls of de Gaulle and Giscard d'Estaing. This was very disadvantageous for France because Germany, which France relied on, could not take any action against the will of the United States. As early as July 1965, the French government was forced to change course. After consulting with the U.S. Treasury, the French Ministry of Finance issued a press release stating that it would postpone discussions on restructuring the international monetary system.

This change in circumstances since mid-1965 is clearly reflected in the evolution of the issue of the creation of international reserve assets in the Ossola (and then Emminger) Committee of the G10. Initially, representatives of the French Ministry of Finance proposed the creation of CRUs guaranteed in gold. The French proposal was that the CRU would be distributed to countries in proportion to their gold holdings and would eventually replace the dollar. The United States initially did not see the need to create an international reserve asset. However, when Fowler took office as Secretary of the Treasury, he began to propose the creation of a reserve asset that was not guaranteed by gold. Other EEC countries agreed with the U.S. proposal, but France objected, arguing that the shortage of international liquidity should be addressed by raising the price of gold and that the new reserve asset should remain a form of credit. However, France's resistance was in vain, and the international reserve assets saw the light of day in July 1969 as a "Special Drawing Right" (SDR) from the IMF, not backed by gold.

The SDR was thus born, as Solomon noted. "For the first time in the history of the world, it is possible to create reserves artificially and on the basis of the decisions of a majority of nations." It paved the way for the "abolition of gold" (Solomon, 1982, pp. 147–148). Solomon, known as a Keynesian, seems to have associated SDRs with the "Bancor" that Keynes once envisioned at the Bretton Woods Conference.

By the way, in September of 1966, when the headwinds against France were growing stronger, Rueff published an article in *Le Monde* entitled "Time for Action" (Rueff, 1966/1980, vol. III-2) where he further refined his concept from a technical point of view and responded to various criticisms of his concept. His response to the criticisms was that they were out of line with the essence of the problem. His response is outlined below.

Several eminent economists, including Robert Triffin and James Tobin, attributed the U.S. reluctance to raise the gold price to political reasons—to avoid benefiting the gold-producing countries of the Soviet Union and South Africa. Since they were U.S. government employees at the time, seconded to the OECD, this may well have been a quasi-official reason given internally by the U.S. government. Rueff, being the theorist that he is, refutes this excuse. In addition to gold, the Soviet Union exports coal, oil, cotton, and other commodities. If the international prices of these exports were to rise, how would the U.S. cope?

The tone of this paper turns pessimistic in the second half. The Western countries will not accept his proposal, he writes, because their governments have ordered their representatives to international organizations not to touch the issue of the gold price. He did not mention his source of information, but it is certain that it came from the French government. Rueff also said that devaluation of the dollar would be politically difficult because the American people would not accept it. "The biggest obstacle, if not the only one, is that American public opinion is opposed to a gold price hike. The only reason the experts are silent on the subject is that they are aware of this public opinion" (Rueff, 1971, p. 141).

Corroborating Rueff's claims, the revaluation of the gold price was completely eliminated from the G10 discussion by the end of 1966. In the United States, as if to replace it, the debate on abolishing gold began to emerge (Institut Charles de

Gaulle, 1992, p. 151). Thus, the United States and EEC countries buried de Gaulle/Rueff's idea. They followed the policy formulated by the U.S. government in 1962, maintaining that the U.S. balance of payments deficit could be eliminated by reducing foreign payments.

8.3.2 SDRs and the Dual Pricing System for Gold—Western Countries Faithfully Practice the Teachings of Russian Revolutionary, Lenin

In 1967, the creation of the SDR, the latter part of a series of measures to create international liquidity, became inevitable. At the same time, however, the U.S. balance of payments deficit was not decreasing, the outflow of gold was not stopping, and inflation was rising. Against the backdrop of this crisis, a gold rush swept through the European markets. On March 17, 1968, the day of the biggest gold rush, a meeting of central bank governors was hurriedly held in Washington. At this meeting, it was decided that the exchange of dollars for gold between the central banks of each country would be conducted at the current official gold price. This was the adoption of the so-called dual price system for gold. At the same time, the gold pool was abolished.

During this period, Rueff continued to lecture and write articles, severely criticizing both the SDR and the dual pricing of gold. His comprehensive article on these two systems, entitled "What Must Happen Will Happen," was published in *Le Monde*, June 4–6, 1969 (Rueff, 1969/1971). The article was also reprinted in newspapers in Britain, Germany, the United States, Japan, Belgium, Greece, Canada, South Africa, and elsewhere. The Japanese newspaper was the *Asahi Shimbun*. So, let's take a look at Rueff's arguments at the time, relying mainly on this article of 1969.

First, with regard to the SDR, Rueff's criticism of it consists of a few main issues. First, this international reserve asset is not a simple credit instrument, but an unquestionable currency. This assessment agrees with Solomon's, but their reasoning differs. Rueff emphasizes the French government's insistence that certain conditions for the use of SDRs be followed, and that this has not been done. These conditions were as follows: that the use of the SDRs should be limited to the repayment of external debt, that the use of the SDRs should be limited to the restoration of equilibrium in the U.S. balance of payments, and that the use of the SDRs should be limited to the confirmation of liquidity shortages in each country.

Second, the biggest beneficiary of the SDR is the United States, which continues to record huge balance of payments deficits. Rueff notes that (1) The criterion for deciding whether to use the SDR is whether the country has a balance of payments deficit, and the SDR has only a limited function as external purchasing power. (2) The SDR is created by the IMF, but the IMF is strongly influenced by the United States.

Third, because of the above, and because SDRs expand the amount of currency in circulation in the creditor countries that receive them, SDRs promote inflation.

Next Rueff critiques the dual pricing system for gold and the abolition of the gold pool. Rueff criticizes these measures as follows: the aim is to force countries that are politically, economically, or militarily dependent on the United States to abandon the exchange of dollars for gold. Therefore, the dual price system for gold is nothing more than "monitored exchangeability," so to speak. Moreover, this system has a major limitation. If the U.S. balance of payments deficit continues to increase, the dollar balance in countries like West Germany will exceed the acceptable limit. As already seen with the repeated speculation on the mark, countries that accumulate dollar balances will be exposed to pressure to raise the parity of their currencies. The only way to alleviate this pressure is to release some of the dollars into the Eurodollar market. According to reliable media reports, this is already being done secretly by West Germany. What's more, there is no guarantee that the creditor countries will continue to comply with the U.S. demands. In the event of a sudden incident, even countries vulnerable to the United States, such as West Germany and Japan, will demand the exchange of dollars for gold, which they are guaranteed as a right.

Thus, Rueff fully rejects the new response to the dollar crisis, the creation of the SDR, and the dual pricing of gold and argues that the catastrophe of the international monetary system is inevitable. But he is not spoon fed and says there is still a solution. The solution, he says, is to shelve part of the dollar balance and convert the rest into gold or other international liquidity. However, prices are higher than they were in 1960, and the price of gold needs to be tripled, not doubled. A tripling of the price would be much more difficult than a doubling, but Rueff says it is not impossible.

It is true that Rueff's discussion of the dollar crisis was wide-ranging. However, at the core of his argument was the following simple statement. If the debtor nation of the United States takes various measures in the name of international cooperation to increase international liquidity without tackling the credit crunch on its own, it will not solve the problem. This is because it will only leave the causes unattended and shift the blame to the creditor countries. "To overthrow the bourgeois system, it is enough to corrupt its currency"—these are the words of the Russian revolutionary Lenin. In the epilogue to his book "The Great Monetary Sins of the Western World" published in 1971, Rueff quoted these words and wrote sarcastically, "The liberal world seems to be faithfully practicing this [Lenin's] teaching" (Rueff, 1971, p. 381).

In August 1976, the United States was finally forced to suspend the exchangeability of gold for dollars. Regardless of whether Rueff's diagnosis of the international currency crisis was correct, there is no doubt that his prediction came true. This was acknowledged by the U.S. government officials.

8.4 Two Remaining Questions

8.4.1 Why Did the US Choose a Floating Exchange Rate System?

In a paper written in October 1963, Robert Roosa wrote that there were two options for an international monetary system other than the gold exchange standard: the gold standard and a floating exchange rate system. The United States gave up the idea of maintaining the gold exchange standard and chose the floating exchange rate system among the remaining options. Moreover, by letting the dollar fluctuate in the exchange market without international consultation, it forced other countries to follow this "system that is not a system", according to Rueff. This is called a policy of "benign neglect."

So why did the United States choose a floating exchange rate system instead of a gold standard? As mentioned earlier, Triffin and Tobin explained that the reason the United States did not adopt the gold standard was that this currency system would benefit the gold-producing countries of the Soviet Union and South Africa. On the other hand, Robert A. Mundell, another economist who was familiar with Rueff's work, spoke at a symposium held in November 1996 to commemorate the 100th anniversary of Rueff's birth and expressed his own views on this point. According to him, the United States was one of the factors that destroyed the gold standard, but "the U.S. did so not out of malice or cruelty, but because of its position as a superpower after the two world wars" (Commissariat Général du Plan, 1997, p. 40). This can be rephrased in Rueff's style as follows. After both world wars, the United States did not raise the gold price of the dollar to avoid deflation in its own economy and the world economy, and it also encouraged inflation by adopting the gold exchange standard. Thus, in short, as a result of the superpowers' choice of policies that thoroughly avoided adjustment, the world suffered two major recessions in the 1930 and 1970s.

Here, I would like to introduce one more interpretation that was shared within the French Ministry of Finance. France's interpretation is an apt example because this country was so determined to maintain the fixed exchange rate system that it continued to hold secret talks with the United States until November 1975. The French interpretation is as follows.

Under a floating exchange rate system, the balance of payments is automatically balanced by changes in the exchange rate, and the domestic economy is also adjusted. In other words, the same effect as that of the gold standard can be achieved. It is true that with the expiration of the Bretton Woods Agreement, the dollar lost its institutional privilege as a reserve currency. Nevertheless, the position of the dollar as a reserve currency and settlement currency is unassailable because of the sheer volume of U.S. international trade and investment. Therefore, the dollar will continue to enjoy reserve currency privileges. Moreover, unlike under the Bretton Woods Agreement, the United States does not have to take responsibility for the stability of the dollar. Furthermore, there is no need to persuade the American people to switch to a floating exchange rate system. A floating exchange rate system was indeed a very convenient system for the U.S. administrators. The United States mobilized major Western countries to rescue the dollar in response to the lack of international liquidity and in the name of international Keynesianism but failed to achieve its own goals. Therefore, the United States turned around and opted for a floating exchange rate system on its own (Gonjo, 2020).

8.4.2 Why Was Rueff Able to Carry His Argument to the End?

Although they never spoke out, many economic and monetary experts seemed to share their views. It is for this very reason that the leading Western media continued to publish his articles. In fact, at the Bank for International Settlements (BIS), known as a forum for international cooperation among central banks, Per Jacobson, the head of Monetary and Economic Department, and other senior officials at the bank, shared the same or similar views as Rueff (Yago, 2015). In his autobiography, Rueff himself also mentioned two of the leading figures who supported him, Etienne Burin des Roziers, the chief of staff of the de Gaulle presidential office, and Maurice Couve de Murville, the then foreign minister and later prime minister, who was known for his economic savvy. He also cites William McChesney Martin, Chairman of the Board of Governors of the U.S. Federal Reserve System, and Robert V. Roosa, Assistant Secretary of the Treasury, as two friends who did not agree to raise the gold price but continued to show "goodwill and respect for my efforts." He also notes that several senior officials of the U.S. monetary authorities "understood and sympathized with my analysis" (Rueff, 1971, pp. 162–163).

It is true that Rueff was not alone. However, he was the only one who openly advocated the restoration of the right to gold and argued for raising the price of gold. He defied not only the French but also the majority of the authorities in the Western world, as well as American public opinion, and continued to argue his case to the end. Why was he able to do this? There are three possible reasons.

The first is Rueff's career as a financial bureaucrat. As described in detail earlier (see Chap. 5), from the time he joined the French Ministry of Finance in the fall of 1923 until World War II, he was an elite bureaucrat in the ministry, wrestling with tense and tumultuous international monetary issues. As a result, he was proud to say that he was more familiar with the international monetary system, especially the mechanism of the gold exchange standard, than anyone else.

The second is that Rueff's economic research was based on an original philosophical and scientific methodology of his own devising. He was not an economist in the narrow sense. As discussed in Chap. 2, according to Rueff, theories in science are formulations of cause–effect relationships that can be observed in nature as laws that humans need. In this respect, there is no difference between economics and natural sciences such as physics. In the same way, according to Rueff, "society is realized and exists by the whole activity of the universe." Thus, an unbalanced economic society that deviates from the theory of economics (i.e., the classical theory) will eventually have to face a catastrophe as long as the individual is guaranteed freedom, i.e., as long as the individual is free to act like a floating gas particle.

The third is his strong sense of crisis with regard to the negative aspects of parliamentary democracy. In his speech in February 1933, he had already raised the issue of the parliamentary system becoming a representative body of private interests, making it difficult to implement policies that were unpopular with the people (see Chap. 11). At the time, however, he was still hopeful that there were intelligent and honorable people in the world. However, since the end of the 1930s, and especially after World War II, when Keynesianism came to dominate national opinion in many countries, Rueff had come to believe that such a person no longer existed. In an interview with the London Economist in February 1965, he said that even under a gold exchange standard, it was theoretically possible to contract the supply of money through credit policy.

> For the past five years, the United States has run a huge balance of payments deficit. What would have been done under the gold standard by an automatic contraction of aggregate demand, the U.S. has not attempted to do by a conscious policy of credit [tightening]. This is proof that such a policy is unworkable. The reason why it cannot be is that no country in a parliamentary democracy can carry out such a difficult policy. The contraction of...aggregate demand is not possible unless it is done automatically, every day, i.e., always in small steps, without anyone noticing (Rueff, 1971, pp. 103–109).

Rueff said that it is precisely because of today's advanced parliamentary democracy that we need to leave it to the "invisible hand," or micro-level coordination. He saw the SDR as a dangerous source of inflation, partly because he saw the IMF as only capable of managing this asset in an inflationary direction.

Interestingly, Keynes, in his last article published in *The Economic Journal* after his death, cautioned against the tendency among economists (neo-Keynesians) to disregard classical theory, saying, that classical theory contains some eternal truths, including the "forces of nature" and even the "invisible hand" that still restores equilibrium today. If we dismiss classical theory, we will be forced to come up with one stopgap measure after another, and equilibrium will never be restored. In this article, Keynes probably wanted to tell the Keynesian admirers that his theory is not a substitute for the forces of nature and the invisible hand.

Keynes's intentions aside, his final message bears a striking resemblance to Rueff's discussion of the dollar and the international monetary system. In his articles and books of the late 1960s, Rueff cited Keynes's last article at least twice as proof that his ideas were not unique (Rueff, 1977, vol. I, p. 292). In the last years of his life, there was a connection between Keynes and Rueff.

Part II
Redefining Liberalism and Neoliberalism

Chapter 9
The Birth of Neoliberalism in Paris, 1938

We return at this point to the pre-World War II era. In August 1938, Walter Lippmann, the famous American columnist known as a libertarian, and author of "The Good Society" (Lippmann, 1938) visited Europe. On this occasion, a symposium of European liberalists, commonly known as the "Lippmann Symposium," was held in Paris from August 26 to 30. A month later, at the end of September, a meeting of the heads of state of Britain, France, Italy, and Germany was held in Munich to discuss Nazi Germany's demand for the annexation of Sudetenland. The Lippmann Symposium took place at a time when Europe was on the verge of a world war. The 5-day symposium was an opportunity for a liberalism that differed in character from the Manchester School liberalism of the nineteenth century, to gain citizenship on the international stage under the name of "neoliberalism."

The one who supported the Lippmann Symposium from a theoretical standpoint was Rueff. At the time, he held the important position of Director General of the Treasury Department at the Ministry of Finance. It was around this time that he shifted the center of his thought from monetary theory to social theory. "Social Order," published in 1945, was the culmination of his new thinking. At the same time, he made neoliberalism his own and theoretically defined the scope of state intervention in the economic and social spheres. In this way, he acquired a policy technology that could meet the social and political demands of his time. This meant that Rueff was on a par with Keynes, although he took a very different approach. After World War II, Rueff worked for the European Court of Justice and made bold proposals for institutional and policy reforms to the government of the day, achieving important results. The theoretical foundation for his success was prepared on the eve of World War II.

The Lippmann Symposium thus marked a major turning point in Rueff's life as a theorist and practitioner (Gonjo, 2006, Chap. 1).

Y. Gonjo et al., *The Truth of Liberal Economy*, Springer Studies in the History of Economic Thought, https://doi.org/10.1007/978-981-99-0841-7_9

9.1 The Lippmann Symposium

The symposium was organized by Louis Rougier, a French philosopher and professor at Grenoble University. He had a wide international network of contacts, including philosophers in Vienna. In the late 1930s, he was involved in the publication of works on liberalism in Paris including French translations of works by Wilhelm Röpke, Friedrich von Hayek, and Lionel Robbins, and the abovementioned work by Lippmann.

Twenty-six libertarians from eight countries participated in the symposium. Among them were prominent economists and philosophers of a relatively young generation, including Röpke, Hayek, Ludwig von Mises, and Michael Polanyi. From France, in addition to Rougier and Rueff, there was the philosopher Raymond Aron, as well as the future Vice President of the European Commission Robert Marjolin, and three innovative business leaders representing the country's electric power, electronics, and aluminum industries.

Liberalism Must Be Renewed and Revised

The Lippmann Symposium opened with keynote presentations by Rougier and Lippmann (*Compte-rendu des séances du Colloque Walter Lippmann,* 1939). The first speaker, Rougier, begins by identifying the current state of decline of liberalism as it is being squeezed by socialism and fascism. According to him, there are two causes for this. The first is that liberalism has been equated with the laissez-faire of the Manchester School. However, liberalism essentially functions within the framework of a legal system created by the state. It differs from laissez-faire because it presupposes legal intervention. However, it is not enough to simply leave the economic problems that actually arise in a liberal society to the legal system and expect that equilibrium will eventually be restored because liberalism must also be able to deal with "short-term" problems, in Keynesian terms. Hence, state intervention in the economy is necessary to an extent and libertarians failed to recognize this. This is the second reason for liberalism's decline.

Based on the above outline, Rougier poses two questions. First, is the decline of liberalism, as Marxism teaches, inevitable because of its own laws of development? Second, is economic liberalism capable of satisfying the social demands of the masses? According to Rougier, liberalism has no future unless it can address these two challenges.

The next speaker, Lippmann, spoke eloquently and passionately about the critical situation facing the Western world, placing it in the context of the history of civilization. According to him, the "century of progress" (the nineteenth century), which was marked by democracy, individualism, economic liberalism, and scientific positivism, has been replaced by an era of war, revolution, and reaction. There is no point in waiting for a revival of the old liberalism of which men like William Gladstone spoke. The situation is imminent. The totalitarian states of Communism, National Socialism, and Fascism are attacking Western civilization, which was formed after more than 2,000 years of severe trials. Lippmann concludes his keynote speech by saying, "The mission of libertarians is not to preach theories that were perfected in the nineteenth century, but to embark on a far-reaching revision of various ideas and to carry on a determined struggle for the defense of civilization."

After the keynote speeches, the discussion was divided into seven sessions according to subjects prepared in advance. Of these, the first and fourth sessions, which dealt with the issues raised by Rougier, were at the core of the discussion.

In the first session, agglomeration and monopoly were the main subjects of discussion. The commentators were generally optimistic about both agglomeration and monopoly. Among them, German-Austrian economists, citing the example of coercive cartels, argued that monopolies are created by the involvement of the state and cannot be a problem without the state's involvement. Mises even says that not all monopolies are bad. Their assessment of agglomeration was even more optimistic. The common perception of the speakers was that agglomeration meant technological progress and development of productive forces and did not in itself mean an immediate retreat from competition.

In the fourth session, the question of "loss" or "pain" caused by economic changes and adjustments to industry and workers was raised, with specific regard to whether liberalism can fulfill its social mission, and whether liberalism can guarantee a minimum cost of living for all.

In relation to the first point. Rueff developed his theory as follows. The reason why people are anxious about their lives is that the economy is not in equilibrium. People's anxiety is a "social expression of economic imbalance." Especially since the depression of 1929, the delay in restoring economic equilibrium has significantly increased social unrest. The delay in restoring equilibrium is due to the lack of adjustment power in today's economic system, especially the adjustment power of money. Since the onset of the depression, efforts have been made to weaken the regulating power of money through such measures as the gold sterilization policy which blocks the link between gold inflows and currency issuance, the generalization of the gold exchange standard, and cooperation among central banks. In addition to money, individual countries have taken a variety of protective measures that have prevented economic readjustment. Thus, according to Rueff, until the economic system regains its regulating power, it will be difficult for liberalism to fulfill its social mission.

The second issue was wages. According to Rueff, as long as the price mechanism is in operation, wages will follow price fluctuations. Also, if the state intervenes to maintain the wage level, unemployment will increase. He goes on to say that people often ask where to find the resources to guarantee a minimum standard of living for workers. This question itself is wrong, he says, because the purpose of an economic system is to pay workers the maximum that is compatible with their productive activities. The correct question to be asked is which is better at achieving this goal, a system that leaves it to the price mechanism or a system that fixes the wage level in advance? Rueff's answer is that "both forms of state intervention in the economic sphere have led only to the impoverishment of the workers."

In this short presentation of the issues, Rueff summarizes the tasks that libertarians need to address as follows. "It is clear that the state must take care of things like education. The real issue is the limits of intervention in a liberal state: what forms of intervention are compatible with the price mechanism?" This report was followed by a series of remarks by economists, but no one disagreed with or elaborated on Rueff's views.

At any rate, the conclusion of the discussions in the two sessions was that liberalism has a future and that its revival is possible.

The Liberal Agenda (The Neoliberal Platform)

On the last day of the symposium, Lippmann read out a draft of a six-point "liberal agenda" that could be called a neoliberal platform. The following is an excerpt of the main points (*Compte-rendu des séances du Colloque Walter Lippmann,* 1939, pp. 99–101).

(1) …Only a price mechanism functioning in a free market can result in an organization of production that allows for the best use of the means of production and the maximum satisfaction of people's desires.
(2) The equilibrium point established in the market is influenced by, and ultimately determined by, the laws governing property rights, contracts, associations and corporations, patents, bankruptcy, currency, banking, and financial systems. The responsibility for determining the legal system that provides the framework necessary for the free development of economic activity rests with the state.
(3) …(abbreviated)…
(4) The purpose of the legal system is to guarantee the maximization of the utility derived from production, subject to constraints determined by other social goals.
(5) The organization of production based on liberal principles does not preclude the deduction of a portion of national income from personal consumption to be applied to the goals of the community. A liberal state can and must take a part of its national income by taxation and apply it to the needs of the community, such as i) National defense; ii) Social security; iii) Social services; iv) Education; v) Academic research.
(6) Thus, liberalism takes as its basic canon the adjustment of production by the price mechanism in the market. However, under the system we want, the following is allowed:

    (a) Market prices are affected by ownership and contracting systems.
    (b) Maximum utility is a social good, but not necessarily the only one that should be pursued.
    (c) Even when production is governed by a price mechanism, the community can be made to bear the expenses incurred in the functioning of that system. In this case, the intervention must act on the causes of the situation to be modified and must not grant the state the means to change individual situations at its discretion.

The neoliberalism defined by the above six points is different from the neoliberalism that is spreading in the world and throughout the United States today. The most notable difference is that the social aspect accounts for a large part of the agenda.

Although the process of drafting the agenda is not clear, there is no doubt that Rueff played a decisive role in the theoretical aspects of the agenda. As proof of this, the draft agenda overlap in many respects with Rueff's remarks at the seminar introduced in the next section.

The reaction of the participants to the draft agenda was all positive. In particular, many appreciated the fact that the basis of liberalism is not utility maximization but the price mechanism, and that it allows for a wide range of state intervention. The draft agenda were thus approved without objection. The discussion on the last day of the symposium concluded with the following words from Rueff: "What was discussed was a question of policy, that is, a question of the rules by which the government should act, not a question of science." In other words, liberalism redefined is solely a matter of state policy, not a revision of (classical) economic theory.

During the symposium, there was also an exchange of ideas about the name of this redefined liberalism. Social liberalism, liberal left, positive liberalism, and neoliberalism were some names that were suggested, but no conclusion was reached. However, after this symposium, the media in continental Europe began to use the term neoliberalism, and many libertarians began to follow suit.

Finally, the symposium closed with the following three resolutions: (1) To establish the International Research Center for the Renewal of Liberalism (hereinafter abbreviated as the "International Research Center") with its headquarters in Paris; (2) To organize branches of the Research Center in the United States by Lippmann, in England by Hayek, and in Switzerland by Röpke; (3) The next international conference was to be held in Paris in 1939, and the topic will be "Forms of Public Power Intervention Compatible with the Price Mechanism," and a report will be requested from Rueff.

9.2 Forms of Public Power Intervention Compatible with the Price Mechanism

The International Research Center was established as planned amidst the heightened military tensions between France and Germany. Its headquarters were located in the Musée Social in Paris, and its president was Louis Marlio, chairman of the L'Aluminium français. The number of members was 48, half of whom were French. Of the non-French members, the majority were Belgians. Among the French members, it should be noted that in addition to Charles Rist and other renowned economists, there were presidents and officers of the French Employers' Federation, ministers of the Popular Front government, and leaders of Socialist Party-affiliated trade unions. Lionel Robbins of the LSE, University of London, who did not attend the symposium, was also a registered member.

The International Research Center was active in organizing seminars and publishing bulletins for a very short time until France and Britain declared war on

Germany in September 1939. Rueff's report, which had been announced at a symposium the previous year, was presented at a seminar organized by the International Research Center in March of the same year.

The Rueff Report—"Liberal Intervention"

In this report, Rueff fully develops his liberal theory, which he had only partially discussed in the previous year's symposium (Rueff, 1939/1967). We can clearly see the characteristics of his theory of state intervention, which would be called "liberal intervention."

Before his main argument, Rueff makes three points. First, an economic organization cannot survive unless it is in equilibrium. Second, the maintenance of economic equilibrium is not based on planning but must be achieved through the price mechanism. Third, the overriding goal of the economic system must be to maximize the well-being of the disadvantaged.

Rueff uses the simplest theoretical model to develop his argument. He describes an economy in equilibrium, where wheat is the only product. In such an economy, a fire destroys part of the wheat crop. The demand for wheat will gradually decrease as people seek alternative products. On the other hand, the price of wheat becomes high, which stimulates people to cultivate uncultivated land and increase wheat planting. Thus, equilibrium is eventually restored. In this model, the price mechanism works perfectly, and it acts to restore the economic equilibrium in response to changes in the environment.

The same situation that arose from the fire can be created by the state. For example, suppose the state dumps wheat into the ocean. In this case, the price mechanism would still work, and equilibrium would be restored. In other words, the price mechanism will work regardless of the environment surrounding it. On the other hand, the price mechanism will not function if there is intervention in the price of wheat, such as keeping the price below a certain level. The economic equilibrium is then blocked and will not be restored as long as the currency remains stable—in other words, as long as the currency does not depreciate.

The same is true when the state intervenes in the labor sphere for humanitarian or social purposes. Changes in working hours act on the supply of labor and thus on the cause of wages. Even if the state shortens the legal working hours and thus reduces the supply of labor, the economic equilibrium will not be compromised if wage determination remains free. Hence, this type of intervention is compatible with the price mechanism.

However, when the wage level is determined by a system of compulsory arbitration or collective bargaining agreements, intervention affects the price itself and unemployment occurs. However, the situation is different when the state provides relief to the unemployed through fiscal measures. If the relief is provided within the framework of a balanced budget, as is the case in the United Kingdom, the imbalance will remain intact. However, bailing out the unemployed by the state means removing a portion of the workforce from the market, which in theory is the same as dumping wheat by the state. Therefore, it can no longer be said that state intervention is incompatible with the price mechanism. On the contrary, if the unemployed are rescued by inflationary means, real wages will fall, and equilibrium will be restored.

Rueff makes the same kind of argument for the realm of tariffs and credit. He concludes that, generally speaking, "interventions that act on the causes of prices" are compatible with the price mechanism, while "interventions that act on prices themselves" are incompatible with the price mechanism.

However, according to Rueff, interventions that are compatible with the price mechanism are not always appropriate. There are two criteria for judging whether an intervention is appropriate or not. One is the "effectiveness" criterion. Family allowances and old-age pensions are necessary, and the state does indeed provide relief to the unemployed for humanitarian and social purposes. Nevertheless, such interventions are only effective if they are "genuine borrowing procedures," i.e., if financing is done through taxation or deductions from personal income through borrowing. Otherwise, inflation will occur, economic equilibrium will be restored in a roundabout way, and the original goal of the state will not be achieved.

The second criterion is the relationship between the "social benefits" of intervention and the "social costs" of intervention. As the history of tariff policy in France shows, when the state intervenes, it tends to emphasize the benefits and ignore the social costs. According to Rueff, this is deceitful and needs to be disallowed by disclosing information about social benefits and costs.

It is clear from the above that for Rueff it is the "form" of intervention that matters, not the weight of intervention. Theoretically, public power can intervene in any way it likes, as long as it does not undermine the price mechanism, and it can help the unemployed and the aged. Rueff himself would later refer to this type of intervention as "liberal intervention."

At the same time, the term "liberal intervention" came to be used by German neoliberals. Typical examples are Franz Böhm, Walter Euken and their group of economists known as the "Old Liberals" or the "Freiburg School." There is a significant difference between their understanding of intervention and Rueff's. For the German school, liberal intervention means the artificial creation by an authoritarian state of the conditions that would be achieved if pure and perfect competition took place within the framework of an impure and imperfect market. This is the so-called policy of "as if" (als ob) (Mirowski and Plehwe, eds., 2009). In the case of Rueff, on the other hand, it means that the state intervenes to change the structure of production and consumption for the general good or to achieve social goals, to the extent that it does not undermine the price mechanism. Also, the means of intervention allowed to the state are limited to taxes and subsidies (Rueff, 1939/1967).

What is the Nature of Liberalism? Is Social Dialogue Possible on the Basis of Neoliberalism?

The first half of the debate was mainly between Rueff and the economist Gaëtan Pirou, and the second half was between Rueff and the socialists (members of the French Socialist Party) and trade union leaders (Rueff, 1939/1967).

The focus of the first half of the discussion was on where to find the essence of liberal theory. While acknowledging the correctness of the theoretical and technical aspects of the Rueff report, Pirou disagreed with its conclusions. This is because the pursuit of maximum utility is the essence of liberalism, and if the social and national perspectives are taken into consideration, the maximization of utility cannot be hoped for. In response, Rueff argues that maximum utility is not a supreme good, and that the essence of liberalism lies in the guarantee of the price mechanism. In other words, he responded with principles 4 and principles 6–8 included in the liberal agenda.

In connection with his rebuttal to Pirou, Rueff explains the need to distinguish between the realm of economics as a science and the realm of policy. In the realm of science, economists must show that economic society can only survive if certain conditions—in Rueff's case, the price mechanism—are met. In the realm of policy, on the other hand, the issue is the goal of the economy and society. This goal is chosen by the will of the people, which is tested in elections. Taking the example of protective tariffs, it belongs to the realm of economics to calculate how much it will cost the people, and it belongs to the realm of policy to decide what to choose based on this information.

Marlio, the director of the International Research Center, who chaired the meeting, took up this explanation by Rueff and said "We are dealing with real problems not only from the point of view of science, but also from the point of view of economic policy. We try to deal with these problems from a human and practical point of view, taking into account the laws that exist and that no one can change." Thus, it can be seen that the functioning of the price mechanism within the institutional framework of reality and the distinction between the realm of "science" and the realm of "policy" were the two things that distinguished neoliberalism, or at least the French school of neoliberalism, from laissez-faire (Bourricaud et Salin, 1989, pp. 93–99).

In the latter part of the discussion with socialists and trade union leaders, the issue of differing perceptions of the current situation arose. For example, Louis Vallon, an engineer and member of a minority group of the French Socialist Party, posed the following question to Rueff: "Today's society is made up of monopolies and cooperatives, and there is no perfect competition. Isn't the price mechanism purely a computational mechanism? Another problem is that there are no social forces that accept liberalism, as both labor and employers are increasingly focused on managing the market."

Rueff refutes this criticism on the basis of his own empirical research and beliefs. Regarding the price mechanism, he cites his own research on the unemployment problem in the United Kingdom in 1950. Drawing on the example of the precise correlation between changes in the unemployment rate and the wage/price index, he argues that the price mechanism is functioning with "extreme precision" and "extreme sensitivity" even in the present age of socialization, and that the price mechanism is not an "ideal image" but a "real image."

Next, Rueff responds to the criticism that there is no such thing as a social force for liberalism. "The only social forces that can move toward the renewal of liberalism are the leftist groups. Perhaps only these groups can understand the true nature of the problems that arise from economic organization, because the only dispute between them and us is over means, not over ends." He called for a "social dialogue" with workers, saying, "I would like to have a great discussion on this point across the table with the representatives of the labor world."

The above report by Rueff and the question-and-answer session surrounding it suggest that Rueff and the International Research Center were trying to achieve cooperation or harmony between liberalists and workers on the basis of neoliberalism. It was only with this intention in mind that the center brought in influential labor and management leaders as members, in addition to researchers, and that the center focused its public relations efforts on diverse social groups.

9.3 The Aftermath of Neoliberalism and the Mont Pèlerin Society

The International Research Center was forced to suspend its activities when France entered the war against Germany and was not able to resume its activities even after the end of the war in 1945 because the prolonged German occupation had left a serious mark in France. During this period, French and Belgian neoliberals, deprived of their freedom, dispersed in search of their own places to live. Rougier, the organizer of the Lippmann Symposium, was expelled from public office after being accused of collaborating with the Vichy government. Furthermore, due to the prolonged lack of investment and renewal of facilities, French industry was in decline across the board, and innovative entrepreneurs could no longer afford to support the International Research Center.

Hayek and Röpke, who were based in England and Switzerland respectively, worked to rebuild the international nexus of their neoliberalism. In 1944, Hayek, with the help of Frank Knight and Aaron Director of the University of Chicago, published a highly successful book, *The Road to Serfdom*, with University of Chicago Press (Hayek, 1944). This led to his being regarded as a standard-bearer for liberalism in both Britain and the United States. Röpke published *Civitas humana*, "The Republic of Freedom" in 1944 (Röpke, 1944), which contributed to the recognition of neoliberalism in the German-speaking world. He was also planning to publish an international journal, for which he was raising funds in Switzerland with the help of businessman Albert Hunold. However, insufficient funds were raised. So Röpke consulted with Hayek, with whom he had been in contact for some time and decided to use the money to establish the International Academy of Political Philosophy, which Hayek had been wanting to establish. Thus, in April 1947, the inaugural meeting of the International Academy of Political Philosophy, which was to be named the "Mont Pèlerin Society," was held in Mont Pèlerin, Switzerland.

The inaugural meeting was attended by 39 people, all of whom were researchers. Sixteen of them were American researchers who attended with the support of American foundations. In contrast, only seven researchers attended the Lippmann Symposium.

Hayek was appointed president of the Mont Pèlerin Society. There were five vice presidents, including Rueff, Knight, and Walter Euken, a representative of the Freiburg School in Germany. The secretariat was divided between Zurich and Chicago, with Hunold in charge of administration (in Zurich) and the director in charge of conferences (in Chicago). The treasurer was Charles Hardy of the Joint Committee on Economic Report (Washington). The Mont Pèlerin Society was registered as a non-profit organization in Illinois in November 1947, with Knight, the director, and Hardy as the incorporators. Its secretariat was located at the University of Chicago. As can be seen from the above organizational structure, the Association was integrated with the University of Chicago in terms of legislation, and Hayek and the three officers living in the United State were in control of the center of the organization. Thus, it can be said that the Mont Pèlerin Society was an American organization while the former International Research Center was a French organization.

There was another major difference between the Mont Pèlerin Society and the former International Research Center. It was conceived as an academic forum that was closed off from the general public. To begin with, the list of invitees to the inaugural meeting prepared by Hayek included only researchers. This was because, as mentioned above, he intended to turn the association into an "International Academy of Political Philosophy."

Hayek's attitude toward the association seems to have been related to his particular view of trade unions. In his keynote speech at the founding meeting, he said: "At the beginning of this century, trade unions were exempted from the common law in many respects....and even violence, intimidation and threats were effectively legalized," and, "If there is any hope for a return to a liberal economy, the question of how to properly limit the power of trade unions in law and in practice is the most important of all questions to which we must pay attention."[1] His tough stance on trade unions was probably owing to factors specific to the Britain environment, rather than the continental European context.

Nonetheless, the directors were divided on the nature of the association. At the first meeting of the Board of Directors, held in Basel on September 19, 1948, an interesting debate ensued.[2] First, the two vice presidents, Euken and Rueff, who were absent from the inaugural meeting and had not heard Hayek's speech, argued that the association should be open to trade union leaders, and that it needed to have a platform. In particular, Rueff went so far as to say that the platform should be "a 'liberal manifesto' that can compete with Karl Marx's manifesto [the Communist Manifesto]" and that it should deal with "the social aspects of liberal economic policy" like the former "liberal agenda." But this was strongly opposed by two American academics as misleading. The problem was that Hayek was reluctant to have a platform, saying he was "hesitant." Thus, the Mont Pèlerin Society was established as an international forum of libertarians without a platform document.

The Mont Pèlerin Society had a serious internal conflict between 1959 and 1961, about which there are many unanswered questions. It is clear, however, that two

---

[1] Hoover Institution Archives (HIA), Hayek papers, Box 71–77.

[2] Hoover Institution Archives (HIA), Hayek papers, Box 80–25.

factors were involved. The first was a rivalry over the management of the association between Hayek, on the one hand, and Hunold and Röpke, on the other, and the second was the widening gap between European and American members over the understanding of neoliberalism. The internal conflicts led to the departure of Röpke and Hunold, who had been instrumental in the founding of the association, and the departure of 17 European members. Euken was already deceased at the time. On the other hand, Rueff, who had a close relationship with Röpke, stayed in the association.

Bertrand de Jouvenel, a French economist who worked with Röpke, spoke frankly about the rift that had developed between European and American members. In a letter he wrote to Milton Friedman dated June 30, 1960, he wrote:

> The Mont Pèlerin Society has gradually turned into a dualism of good and evil, in which the state can do no good and private enterprise can do no evil. I do not feel comfortable with members impeaching virtually everything that has been accomplished in our time in the name of an imaginary 19th century....This group is not a free gathering of people who think together about the basic agreements of the founding. It is a team of fighters (cited in Mirowski and Plehwe, eds., 2009).

This letter shows that members living in the United States, who accounted for about 30% of the membership at that time, were openly advocating a form of liberalism no different from the Manchester School of the nineteenth century, and that tensions were growing between the European members, especially those in continental Europe.

From the end of the 1970s, the term "neoliberalism" came into common use in the media as Prime Minister Margaret Thatcher, influenced by Hayek and Friedman, promoted drastic reforms in Britain. At the same time, neoliberalism became associated with the Chicago School of economics and tended to be equated with market fundamentalism. This development is understandable if we consider the fact that Hayek and the members of the Mont Pèlerin Society living in the United States were cautious if not negative about redefining neoliberalism.

Finally, let me emphasize that the neoliberalism which had its origins in the Lippmann Symposium did not disappear with the cessation of the International Research Center and the appearance of the Mont Pèlerin Society.

The "liberal agenda" was reflected in the Düsseldorf Platform (July 1949) of the Christian Democratic Union (CDU), the leading political party in West Germany, as early as after World War II. In an article published in June 1953, Rueff analyzed this platform and described it as being the same as the neoliberalism they had launched (Rueff, 1953/1980, vol. III-2, pp. 69–70). The use of the term "social market economy" in the Dusseldorf Platform meant that in West Germany neoliberalism would henceforth be known as the social market economy and would become the basic philosophy underpinning the country's economy and society. In France after World War II (see Chap.12), neoliberalism was also inherited, albeit with some twists and turns, through Rueff's participation in various forums and the fiscal and economic structural reforms in which he was involved.

Besides these examples of Germany and France, this form of neoliberalism remained alive as a supporting philosophy in the integrated Europe that originated in the 1950s (see Chap. 11). In fact, the Treaty of Lisbon, an amendment to the European Constitutional Treaty that entered into force in December 2009, stipulates the German-derived "social market economy" as the EU's philosophy.

Chapter 10
The World of Rueff's "Social Order"—The Economic Sociology of Anti-inflation

From the beginning of the 1920s, Keynes made a number of statements that seemed to be in favor of inflation. In his "General Theory" of 1936, he proposed a strict definition of inflation and clarified his position on it. He called the phenomenon in which prices rise due to further expansion of the quantity of money in a state of full employment "genuine inflation," and criticized the popular understanding of inflation that regarded general increases in the quantity of money as inflationary. However, Keynes's definition of inflation came to be known to the general public as a simplification that accepted aggressive fiscal stimulus and the resulting increase in money supply and prices. Keynesian theory attracted attention in the 1930s in Western countries suffering from recessions and was enthusiastically supported by policymakers in many countries during the economic recovery period after World War II. This was due to both Keynes's original understanding of inflation and its popular interpretation.

As François Perroux's memorandum shows (see Chap. 6), Keynesian theory was generally understood as "a theory of development, growth, and booms" from early on after World War II. Once the postwar reconstruction was over, Keynesian theory was treated as an integral part of growth theory by policymakers. This is because if aggregate demand policy allows the economy to grow without painful adjustments or structural reforms, the fruits of growth for each social category will be uniformly greater. As a result, people will be less concerned about distributional issues, and social peace will be easier to achieve. Thus, a policy theory that places growth as the overriding social goal, instead of full employment, gradually emerges. However, this policy theory also took for granted the continuation of investment and the accompanying inflation in the name of "managed inflation." The "stop-and-go" policies implemented in the United Kingdom and France illustrate this point well.

In contrast, the neoliberals, whether they were continental European economists or the economists of the Mont Pèlerin Society and its circle, were all anti-inflationary, unlike Keynes and the growth theorists who emerged after his death. However, no other economist seems to have developed an in-depth argument as to why inflation should be rejected. In his magnum opus, "The Social Order," Rueff argues that

Y. Gonjo et al., *The Truth of Liberal Economy*, Springer Studies in the History of Economic Thought, https://doi.org/10.1007/978-981-99-0841-7_10

inflation violates individual freedom and disrupts the order of civilized society, and thus condemns it. In this book, he also presents an original theory that shares some similarities with economic sociology.

10.1 "False Rights" and "True Rights"

The philosopher Bergson wrote in his book "Creative Evolution": "The way events are ordered is precisely proportional to the degree to which they satisfy our thoughts. In other words, order is a kind of harmony between subjects and objects. It is a spirit that rediscovers itself in things" (Bergson, 1923, p. 242). From this definition of order by Bergson, Rueff derives the proposition that "to order society is to fit it into the plan that our spirit desires" (Rueff, 1946/1967, p. 192). Incidentally, Rueff's plan is a carefully formulated and ordered whole that concerns all members of society equally.

Rueff's "Social Order" is dedicated to showing what this whole picture of ordering society looks like. More specifically, he uses two operative concepts, "false rights" and "true rights," to show how society is ordered and maintained by each political system that has emerged in history. These two concepts appear repeatedly throughout "Social Order" and are the so-called leitmotifs of the book. Rueff often summarized the contents of "Social Order" in his lectures and in his autobiography. I will now examine his arguments with reference to these summaries.

According to Rueff, the most general right of man is the right of ownership over what is commonly called "wealth" and is the object of desire. Article 544 of the French Civil Code, which originated from the Code Napoléon (enacted in 1803), the world's first modern civil code, defines property rights as follows: "the power to set at one's disposal a thing exclusively, without restriction by law or regulation." According to Rueff, two conditions are necessary for this kind of ownership to have any real meaning.

The first is the legal system. Things as wealth are finite, and there are people other than the owner who wish to enjoy these things. Therefore, the right of ownership has no real meaning unless it can exclude others who are competing for the enjoyment of the thing. For this reason, it is necessary to establish penalties and to eliminate non-owners by force. This is why the police exist. In other words, "the essential nature of property rights is that they provide a basis for allowing police intervention" (Rueff, 1981, vol. IV, p. 95).

By the way, the content of ownership is not the "thing" itself, but the "ability" to enjoy and freely dispose of the thing. In other words, ownership is a "container," so to speak, in which wealth, the thing, is stored. On the other hand, the value of the wealth stored in this container is expressed in terms of price. This is ownership from an economic perspective. Such ownership is meaningless unless the thing (wealth) in the "container" can always be freely exchanged for other things (wealth) with different use-values. This requires that when the owner of a thing (hereinafter called the "right holder") wants to replace it with another thing, the thing he wants to get instead must surely exist as an equivalent demand. Such a condition can only be guaranteed by the existence of a free market with a functioning price mechanism. This is because in a market, the prices of goods supplied to the market fluctuate constantly, and they are finally adjusted to the level of demand to establish an equilibrium point. When such a market exists, the ownership of the right holder becomes an inherent right, or "true right." Therefore, the existence of a free market with a functioning price mechanism is the second condition for property rights to have a real meaning.

When this second condition is deficient, ownership becomes a "false right." For example, if the price of a thing supplied to the market is maintained in a forcible way at a level above the equilibrium point, the quantity of rights that the right holder is willing to exchange for other things will exceed the quantity of rights he expected to have during the same transaction period. In that case, there will be no buyers for some of the things supplied to the market. The rights that the right holder can freely dispose of become false, or "false rights," to the extent that there is no buyer. This is the case when wages remain above the level that guarantees equilibrium in employment according to the provisions of labor laws, or when wages are fixed according to collective agreements. In either case, the price mechanism does not work in the labor market, so some of the rights of the suppliers (sellers) of labor become "false rights" and unemployment occurs.

Thus, whether property rights become "true rights" or "false rights" depend on whether there is a free market. Moreover, it is often the case that state intervention in the market creates "false rights."

10.2 Financial Claims and the Manipulation of "False Rights" by the State

There is a special kind of ownership in property rights: claims, or ownership of claims. According to Rueff, claims occupy a special position among ownership rights because they are securitized and circulated as financial bonds, and their volume is large, and only the state can manipulate the "false rights" that arise from bond issuance. Here again, the state is deeply involved in the creation of "false rights."

The state issues government bonds in order to cover its budget deficit. This act of the state creates "false rights." This occurs in two ways. In the first, the state forces the central bank to underwrite the bonds at a price above the market price, and in the second, the central bank purchases the bonds on the open market at a price above the market price. In either case, there is an increase in the issuance of currency and the currency depreciates. Thus, some of the goods supplied to the market are no longer available to buyers, and a "false right" is created. According to Rueff, this is how most inflation occurs. If inflation continues under the gold standard, gold will eventually flow out of the central bank, until finally the nation will have to decide to stop using the gold standard. On the other hand, if the gold standard has already been suspended and fiat money is in circulation, prices will soar and the currency will depreciate in the currency markets.

As it happens, states try to hide their budget deficits because they are afraid that the deficits will damage the value of their currency, which in turn will confuse the society. There are two ways to do this. One is the liberal way, which is to raise taxes. The other is the authoritarian method of changing the use of money by property owners to conform to the will of the state. Typical examples are price controls, rationing, exchange controls, and bilateral exchange clearing systems. In practice, since the budget deficit cannot be covered by tax increases alone, the two methods are usually implemented simultaneously. However, there are limits to the effectiveness of this, and eventually the state will resort to authoritarian methods alone.

As is clear from the above, "false rights" arise through a variety of circuits. But whatever the circuit, they all have one thing in common: they arise from the undermining of free market functioning, and the state is often deeply involved in this.

In a society ruled by "false rights," the most common human right, the right of ownership, is violated, and social chaos ensues. Eventually, the public authorities cannot leave the chaos unattended and try to restrict the exercise of the rights of property owners through the price controls and rationing systems mentioned above. Thus, people are deprived of their freedom. The legal system was developed in order to prevent such a situation from occurring. Rueff wrote: "The legal system is the invisible foundation of human freedom. Whoever harms it, regardless of his motives, commits an inexplicable crime, a crime against human dignity" (Rueff, 1977, vol. I, p. 190). Rueff saw human freedom, property rights and the price mechanism that guarantees them, and the legal system as mutually inseparable. It was precisely this understanding of liberalism that led Rueff to criticize Keynes so harshly and to serve as a judge on the Court of Justice of the European Coal and Steel Community (ECSC) and the European Economic Community (EEC).

Importantly, Rueff's theory of inflation arising from budget deficits is based on the realities of small and medium-sized industrial countries like the European countries during the interwar period and after World War II until the end of the 1960s. It assumes an economy that is essentially complete within the framework of a traditional national economy built on industry and international trade, and one with a relatively small GDP. As the international movement of capital becomes more common under a floating exchange rate system and economic globalization progresses, budget deficits will not necessarily be directly linked to inflation. In addition to budget deficits, other factors that cause inflation will also emerge. Nevertheless, if the problem is narrowly limited to the level of a single country, budget deficits remain the most fundamental factor in inflation.

10.3 Economics is not a Science of Wealth

As mentioned, Rueff's "Social Order" is built on the foundation of monetary and social theories. In this regard, his attitude is very different to the Anglo-Saxon economists' view. In his autobiography published in 1977, the last year of his life, he wrote that Economics "is not a science of wealth.…It is a science of the relation between certain things which some people want and all the people who want them." He also wrote: "In primitive society there are no economic relations in which each individual defines for himself a sphere of enjoyment and control. Economic relations, on the other hand, come into being only when a meritocracy, a police force organized and steered by social power, guarantees the exclusive enjoyment of goods [wealth] by a few" (Rueff, 1977, vol. I, p. 182).

So, what is economics? Rueff answers, "Economics is like a little outgrowth of the legal system that enforces social peace. Without the police and the legal system, there would be no exchange, no gifts, no loans, no wage labor. There would be only terrible violence and arbitrariness. Economics is half-embedded in the legal system, so to speak, and cannot be said to be an independent science" (Rueff, 1977, vol. I, p. 182).

The theory that Rueff arrived at through writing "The Social Order" is clearly different in character from the tradition of economics in Anglo-Saxon countries since Adam Smith. It can be called both an economic and a social theory. In the 1930s, he had begun to write a book on the dynamics of money, as a sequel to his previous book on the statics of money (i.e. "The Theory of Monetary Phenomena"). On completing it in 1945 he aptly titled it "Social Order" since it spans both monetary theory and sociology. "Social Order" came to be the publication most representative of Rueff's contribution. In essence, unlike Keynes, Rueff did not develop a stand-alone system of economics. For Rueff, "[e]conomics cannot be said to be an independent science" which is also why, at a seminar of the International Research Center for the Renewal of Liberalism in September 1939 (see Chap. 9), he was able to argue that the essence of liberalism is not the realization of maximum utility but the guarantee of the functioning of the price mechanism.

Besides Rueff, Euken, Röpke, Hayek, and other influential neoliberals in and from continental Europe, did not try to build their own economics, or "science of wealth." This may be because they had an economic and social philosophy similar to that of Rueff.

Rueff's understanding of economics may give the impression that he saw a static economic society as the way society should be, when in fact, this was not the case. As will be discussed in detail (see Chap. 12), in July 1960, in a report for a government committee, Rueff outlined the policy stance that France should take: Eliminate the various regulations so that the price mechanism can function at full capacity. This will lead to the emergence of a dynamic society in which the economic structure is constantly renewed, and people's living standards will improve. This is the kind of society that France should aim for. In short, he had in mind a society where there was no inflation, and where economic development was the norm—incidentally, Rueff himself never used the term "growth."

Chapter 11
European Economic Integration and Neoliberalism

In April 1929, while on secondment to the League of Nations Secretariat in Geneva, and at the request of the French Ministry of Foreign Affairs, Rueff wrote a memorandum that could be considered one of the main origins of the Rome treaty of 1957. Thereafter, whenever the European economy entered a critical phase, he made public his noteworthy views on the theoretical and practical significance of creating a "Common Market" in Europe, where goods, capital, and people could move freely, and recommended the principles that would support this market.

Rueff is not the only economist who has argued for the benefits of creating a regional market in Europe. Since the 1920s, there have been a number of proposals for regional integration in Europe, and organizations have been formed to realize them. However, no other economist has developed a coherent and realistic theory of regional economic integration from such an early stage as Rueff has. This is not only because he was an outstanding theorist but also because he had been present at several international conferences which all ended poorly.

Rueff's various projects on a Common Market led to a series of realizations after World War II. First, in April 1951, France, Germany, Italy, and the Benelux countries signed the Treaty of Paris, creating the European Coal and Steel Community (ECSC). Then in March 1957, the same six countries signed the Treaty of Rome, creating the European Economic Community (EEC) and the European Atomic Energy Community (EURATOM). The ECSC aimed to create a joint market for coal and steel, the EEC a joint market for products other than coal and steel in general, and EURATOM a joint market for materials and equipment necessary for the development of nuclear energy. (EURATOM, however, carried out very limited activities).

With the birth of these communities, the political and economic tensions that had dominated the European countries would essentially disappear in the western half of Europe. This indeed marked a new era for Europe. Rueff became the first judge of the Court of Justice of the three communities and devoted the last 10 years of his professional life to this position.

Y. Gonjo et al., *The Truth of Liberal Economy*, Springer Studies in the History of Economic Thought, https://doi.org/10.1007/978-981-99-0841-7_11

Interesting points of comparison may be made with regard to the community and the Common Market in relation to Keynesian theory and neoliberalism. Basically, the EEC's Common Market becomes unsustainable when there is a widening gap between the fundamental economic conditions (fundamentals) of the sovereign member countries, especially the rate of price increases and the rate of budget deficits. If the divergence exceeds a certain limit, exchange rates among the member countries within the region become strained, and the free movement of goods, capital, and people within the Common Market becomes impossible. Therefore, bringing economic policies of member countries closer to each other, (i.e., "convergence" in the terminology of the Community), is essential for the existence of the Common Market. This means that the Common Market is in principle incompatible with a Keynesian approach, which allows governments in underemployed countries to pursue discretionary policies, most notably deficit financing and inflationary policies. The history of the development of the EEC coincides with the history of the elimination of Keynesianism from the countries of the region, and this was no accident (Gonjo, 2013).

Second, both the ECSC and EEC Common Markets are artificial markets created by political agreement between sovereign states. They are free competitive markets, but their functioning is guaranteed by the legal system, and the intervention of public authorities is allowed as long as it does not interfere with the functioning of the market. Therefore, according to Rueff, a Common Market is the very embodiment of neoliberalism as defined by the Lippmann Symposium.

11.1 The Idea of a European Common Market

11.1.1 Briand's Concept of a "European Union" and Rueff's Concept of an "Economic Treaty"

On September 5, 1929, the French Minister of Foreign Affairs, Aristide Briand, addressed the General Assembly of the League of Nations and expressed his support for the establishment of a "federalist relationship" among European countries. Briand's famous vision of a "European Union" is the vision presented in this speech and in the memorandum prepared by Briand's office, which will be discussed later. It will become clear in this chapter that this concept was based on Rueff's idea of a Common Market.

On September 9, 4 days after Briand's speech, the European countries agreed that France would begin to work on the concept of Briand's speech, and the French government entrusted this task to Alexis Léger (pseudonym Saint-John Perse), a poet (and later Nobel laureate) who worked in Briand's office. Léger summarized the results of his work in a "Memorandum on the Organization of the European

Federal System" dated May 1, 1930,[1] and submitted it to the League of Nations on behalf of the French Ministry of Foreign Affairs. What is noteworthy about this memorandum is that it proposes the creation of a "Common Market" to achieve coordination in the economic sphere, based on the basic recognition that the critical situation threatening the peace of Europe was caused by the "uncoordination" seen in the European economy in general." The contents of the proposal can be summarized in the following five items.

(1) Establish the general principles of the EPA as the political responsibility of each government.
(2) On the basis of the Treaty, a Common Market for the free movement of goods, capital and people will be established between European countries. The technical aspects necessary to achieve this goal will be left to a committee of experts.
(3) The establishment of a Common Market will be carried out progressively.
(4) The establishment of a Common Market will be pursued in cooperation with and in the spirit of the League of Nations.
(5) Matters related to national defense are excluded from the scope of the treaty.

What is particularly striking about this vision is the concrete way in which the Common Market is to be realized, particularly the way in which it is to be created step-by-step under political supervision. This top-down approach to integration would require the creation of a state-like structured organization of the countries involved. Therefore, it can be said that the memorandum compiled by Léger anticipated the creation of institutions such as the European Council and the European Commission, which would later be established under the Treaty of Rome, although this was not explicitly proposed.

In September 1928, 1 year before the Briand speech, at the time of the League of Nations General Assembly, Rueff exchanged opinions with Léger regarding his idea of an international economic treaty. Léger asked Rueff to summarize this idea in a memorandum by April 1929 and Rueff subsequently prepared a memorandum entitled "Economic Treaty" (Rueff, 1929/1979, vol. III-1) and delivered it to Léger. The title "Economic Treaty" was a reference to the Briand/Kellogg Treaty ("Non-war Treaty") signed in August 1928, which was meant to be an international treaty to put an end to the conflict between European countries over tariffs, an economic version, that is, of the Non-war Treaty.

The main body of this memorandum consisted of six articles, with the following explanation attached: At the International Economic Conference held under the auspices of the League of Nations in May 1927, the issue of tariffs was discussed, and the report of the conference stated that the countries should cooperate in reducing tariff rates. This recommendation, however, was never acted upon. The governments of the countries did not take direct responsibility for responding to the recommendations, leaving it to a deliberative body of experts. Moreover, the members of the

[1] Ministry of Foreign Affairs, *Memorandum on the Organization of a System of Federal European Union,* 1 May, 1930, World Digital Library.

deliberative body included representatives of industry associations and their officials. As a result, the report of this body was heavily influenced by individual interests, and the status quo was maintained. The purpose of this six-article economic treaty is to ensure that the tariff issue is finally resolved without making the same mistake.

Significantly, the six articles in Rueff's memorandum are the same as the description of the Common Market in the memorandum by Léger. If we take this fact and the background to the formation of the Léger memorandum into account, we can confidently say that the Léger memorandum was a rewrite of the Rueff memorandum to fit the format of the Foreign Ministry document. In addition, Briand's speech at the League of Nations General Assembly in 1929 too was based on the Rueff/Léger concept.

11.1.2 "Some Insanity Raging in the World"

In February 1933, an ad hoc "Peace School" was held at the Sorbonne University. Rueff gave a long lecture here, moderated by Charles Rist, entitled "Some Insanity Raging in the World." The year 1933 was the last year of Rueff's service in London, so this lecture was his last opportunity to speak his mind relatively freely in public.

At the time, a recession was sweeping the world, and European countries were all focusing on increasing protectionist trade. Fascism was on the rise in the countries bordering France, and international tensions were rising. Unlike in 1928–29, the situation was no longer idealistic. In his lectures at the Sorbonne, Rueff used the more modest term "free trade area" instead of "Common Market" and stated: "The more the area in which goods circulate freely expands, the greater will undoubtedly be the interests of the liberal system. Therefore, I would like the 'free trade' zone to be as large as possible. I firmly believe, however, that even a modest amount of 'free trade' is better than none" (Rueff, 1933/1979, vol. III-1, p. 312).

But Rueff believes that even a modest free trade zone is not forthcoming. The prime ministers, ministers of economy and commerce, as well as economic bureaucrats, all speak in favor of liberal tariff policies at international conferences. However, when they return to their home countries, they accept the demands of industry groups and proceed to raise tariff rates and strengthen the quota system for imports in the name of eliminating the trade deficit and protecting domestic industry. In addition, various protectionist trade arguments are gaining momentum, and public institutions are more or less influenced by these arguments. According to Rueff, this situation is due to the fact that government officials do not have a proper understanding of economic issues. He will spend most of his talk correcting the fallacies in the popular understanding of trade deficits and the balance of payments, as well as the fallacy of protectionist trade advocacy.

The first issue Rueff addressed in his lecture was the question of why government officials' words and actions differ so much from those of their foreign and domestic counterparts. According to him, it is because they are caught up in the heavy commercialism that regards a trade deficit as a loss of national wealth. It is true that in the interwar period, the concept of balance of payments was still unknown to the general public, and there were no official statistics on the non-trade balance or capital account. This is why, for example, in France, even in the 1930s, official reports ignored the existence of other balance of payments items and simply equated the balance of trade with the balance of payments. Rueff sees this as the root of the problem. He explains that the balance of payments is balanced through changes in the trade balance, the non-trade balance, and the capital account (unless there is an anomaly such as a flight of capital out of the country), and that it is not possible to change a trade deficit into a surplus by policy. He goes on to say that the adoption of special protectionist policies, such as import quotas and exchange controls, will not fundamentally change the problem. This is because, under a liberal system, the economy is constantly being adjusted at the micro-level and cannot be managed by the authorities. Needless to say, this is the same argument that Rueff used in his criticism of Keynes in the transfer debate.

Thus, the conclusion that Rueff drew was the exact opposite of the current theory. In other words, not only in theory but also in the light of the historical experience of France and England since the end of the nineteenth century, the deficit in the balance of trade does not indicate poverty, as is claimed, but on the contrary, it indicates affluence.

Next, Rueff severely criticizes the equilibrium tariff theory that justifies protectionist trade, and the protectionist trade theory to secure employment, as they ignore the serious negative effects of protection. The negative effects include, for example, hindering competition, delaying the adoption of new technologies and the efficiency of production organizations, and hindering the inter-sectoral movement of labor, which in turn makes it impossible to achieve the social goals of increasing productivity and raising living standards. Furthermore, Rueff emphasizes that European countries, which are all small, can benefit greatly from foreign trade, unlike the United States, which is a large country with a large land area, a variety of resources, and diverse industries.

After the above discussion, Rueff suggests concrete ways to create a free trade zone. First, the reduction of tariff rates should be implemented uniformly and with the same reduction for all sectors, without any preference among the production sectors. This is because there is no such thing as a rational tariff system, and the tariff system that exists today has been shaped by history. This is also because protective tariffs have the effect of raising the cost of production for all production sectors, including those that are not subject to protection. The second point to keep in mind is to minimize the pain that the "adjustment" associated with tariff reduction brings to society and to individuals.

After confirming these two points, Rueff proposes that the current tariff rate of 30% be reduced by a uniform one percent every year to complete the free trade zone in 30 years. Incidentally, the Treaty of Rome, signed a quarter of a century later, adopted the same idea. However, in the Treaty of Rome, the elimination of intra-regional tariffs is to be completed within 12 years, not 30 years.

At the end of the lecture, Rueff raises the issue of the role of the state. According to him, the modern state has a mission to serve the "general interest." This mission is generally understood to be to scoop up individual interests as much as possible and reflect them in state policies. However, this understanding is not correct because "the general interest is not the sum of individual interests." What the state should do is the opposite. Rueff says: "A state that serves the general interest must stubbornly resist the individual demands emanating from all sectors of the state."

In any countries, however, the parliamentary system has become a mere system of interest representation, making it difficult for the state to resist individual demands. Rueff acknowledges this fact. But he does not give up hope that there are intelligent and honorable people in the government and in the private sector. The lecture at the Sorbonne concluded with the following words: "To resist the pressures of the economic demagogue, we must first and foremost have grounds for resistance….I have spoken to you this evening about this basis" (Rueff, 1979, vol. III-1, p. 316).

11.2 The European Common Market as the Arrival Point of Neoliberalism

11.2.1 The European Common Market is an "Institutional Market"

Between the eve of the signing of the treaty of Rome in 1957 and early 1958, Rueff gave two lectures on the relationship between the Common Market and institutions and published three articles. In April 1964, he gave a lecture in Cologne, Germany to commemorate the tenth anniversary of the founding of the Community Court of Justice, and the manuscript of this lecture was published in a commemorative volume entitled "The Court and Political Economy" (Rueff, 1979, vol. III-1). There is a great deal of literature on communities and markets, but none of it discusses the reality of their institutions and operations from the perspective of economic theory and thought. For this reason, Rueff's papers are invaluable.

According to Rueff, the essential feature of the Common Market is that it is an artificially constructed market among the six countries of continental Europe. In order for such a wide-area market to function, it is not enough to decide to remove the various obstacles (tariffs, cartels, various subsidies, etc.) that hinder free economic activity through international treaties. Therefore, the Treaty of Paris and the Treaty of Rome provided for the establishment of the Supreme Body, the Council of Ministers and the Court of Justice in the case of the ECSC, and the Council of Ministers, the European Commission and the Court of Justice in the case of the EEC. However, Rueff interprets the term "institutions" used in the two treaties to include not only these bodies but also the rules and precedents that order the relations between states, companies, and individuals in the Common Market.

Rueff focuses on the above characteristics of the Common Market and characterizes the ECSC and EEC as "institutional markets." This is because the Common Market is a free market with a functioning price mechanism, but such a function is guaranteed by the legal system. In Germany, there is a trend of neoliberalism called "Ordoliberalism." As already mentioned (see Chap. 9, Sect. 2), this trend has the idea that public power creates the market that should exist, and the market that should exist is called the "as if" market. Roughly speaking, the institutional market is a kind of "as if" market.

There are two distinctive features of the ECSC and EEC as institutional markets. The first is that these markets are not what the old, naive libertarians like the Manchester School of the nineteenth century thought they were. For the Manchester School, the market is a spatially expanded version of the rural market, in which public institutions do not intervene. However, in the case of the Common Market, which is an institutional market, intervention is possible as long as it is of a type that does not undermine the price mechanism. Therefore, the philosophy that supports the Common Market is none other than the neoliberalism that was launched at the Lippmann Symposium in 1938. Rueff writes:

> The institutional market is the culmination and completion of the movement for the renewal of liberal thought that emerged 20 years ago under the names of neoliberalism, social liberalism, and even liberal socialism. In the course of this movement's development, the desire for an institutional market and the realization that there is a way to achieve such a desire finally led to ECSC Formula (*formule*), or the method of community. This method will be applied to all production sectors in the EEC in the future (Rueff, 1979, vol. III-1, p. 352).

Furthermore, Rueff cleverly uses a metaphor to explain the difference between the old liberalism and their own neoliberalism in terms of institutions. For the old liberals, freedom is a "state of nature." In fact, Jean-Jacques Rousseau wrote at the beginning of the first chapter of the first volume of "The Social Contract" (1762). "Man is born free. But everywhere he is in chains" (Rousseau, 1896, p. 10). If one understands freedom as Rousseau does, then to regain lost freedom, one need only remove the obstacles that deprived one of it. But the neoliberals don't see it that way. Freedom has been acquired gradually over thousands of years through terrible and painful interventions on the religious, moral, political, and social fronts, and freedom is always in danger of being lost. To quote Rueff: "Contrary to Rousseau, the neoliberals believe that the majority of people were born in chains, and only the progress of institutions can free them from these chains. The progress of institutions has only partially freed the people from their chains" (Rueff, 1979, vol. III-1, pp. 352–353).

Another outstanding feature of the ECSC and EEC as institutional markets is that they are supported by a thoroughgoing realism. This is well illustrated by two facts.

First, they are limited in scope both geographically and economically. The reason for this is that the establishment of an institutional market requires a political agreement among the countries involved. This is the reason why the geographical scope of the two European Common Markets is limited to six countries. It is also why the first ECSC joint market was limited to coal and steel because these were the only two products for which a political agreement among the six countries was possible in 1951.

Secondly, safeguards are allowed in the EEC Common Market. In addition, the agricultural sector is subject to special protection, separate from the manufacturing sector. This special protection is guaranteed by the Common Agricultural Policy.

Under the Common Agricultural Policy, the prices of agricultural products in the region are controlled by the Community, and each product is distributed within the region at a single price and without exchange rate risk (up to 1.5%, which existed even under the Bretton Woods fixed exchange rate system). Such a system was established in order to reach a political agreement among the six countries due to the special circumstances of agricultural production. Thus, the six countries of continental Europe chose "partial laissez-passer" instead of "full laissez-passer" and "partial laissez-faire" instead of "full laissez-faire". Rueff explains this choice by the six countries by quoting a proverb from the Arab world: "If you want your luggage to be carried, a living goat is still better than a dead horse" (Rueff, 1979, vol. III-1, p. 350).

The ECSC and EEC will eventually merge to become the EC (European Community). The EC then evolved into the EU (European Union). However, the foundation of any integrated Europe was the Common Market (called the "single market" since the 1980s). When the floating exchange rate system spread throughout the world in the 1970s, European countries set the goal of integrating their currencies in order to protect the Common Market. First, they launched the snake, then the EMS (European Monetary System), a system to limit the fluctuation of currencies among European countries to a narrow range. Finally, the single currency, the euro, is introduced, and the national currencies used by each country are abolished. This was a shift to a currency system that could be called the ultimate fixed exchange rate system, which could not be achieved even under the classical gold standard. Both systems were established on the basis of a political agreement among the states in the region and were administered by the various institutions of an integrated Europe. Thus, from an economic point of view, integrated Europe has been, to this day, the very embodiment of neoliberalism, or an "institutional market," as Rueff calls it.

In describing the basic features of the Common Market as an institutional market, officials involved in the operation of the European institutions sometimes use the predicates "communal," "communal method," or "cooperation," thereby suggesting that various institutions and mechanisms are in place to alleviate the pain that the free competitive market of the Common Market brings to the economies and societies of the member countries, and to reconcile the conflicts of interest that arise among the nations. In fact, this means that an integrated Europe has been consistently established on the basis of communal relations since the ECSC and EEC, at least until the establishment of the EU.

11.2.2 The Issue of Britain's EEC Membership and the "Institutional Market"

In 1963, Britain's first application to join the EEC had been rejected by French President Charles de Gaulle. In May 1964, Rueff prepared a short memorandum (unpublished) (Rueff, 1979, vol. III-1, p. 332) in which he gave a brief but interesting thought on the issue of Britain's accession to the EEC, as follows:

The United Kingdom did not join the ECSC or the EEC. Instead, in May 1960, it took the initiative to launch the European Free Trade Association (EFTA) with six other countries that were not members of the EEC, based on a customs union and a Common Market, but with common policies in the three sectors of trade, agriculture, and transport that considered the particular circumstances of each sector and member country. In addition, the EEC was supposed to implement such institutions and policies. Moreover, the EEC aimed to gradually deepen these institutions and policies. This international integration organization was literally a "communal" political alliance. The EFTA, on the other hand, was merely a simple free trade area that abolished only internal tariffs. In this way, the United Kingdom had an economic integration concept that differed in character from that of the continental European countries, but as the EEC began to function smoothly and produce results, it began to desire membership in the EEC. At the same time, there was a movement in and around the British government to reorganize the EEC in line with British interests in the name of "renegotiation."

Rueff wrote the following about this issue of Britain's membership in the EEC: Britain's membership is desirable. But it must be guaranteed on the condition that the existing EEC, "a strongly integrated community with effective institutions," can be maintained. The question, for Rueff, is whether Britain will accept the minimum level of integration necessary for the survival of the community. This rather roundabout and skeptical expression suggests that Rueff saw that it would not be easy for Britain to come to terms with the institutional policies that made up the community and the political circumstances of the continental European countries that needed them. According to Rueff's discussion of institutional markets in the previous section, the Common Market is based on the idea of continental European neoliberalism, a neoliberalism that is compatible with communal relations. Rueff, who had spent a long period of time in London and was familiar with British culture and thought, is thought to have been well aware of the fact that there was a gap that could not be easily bridged between the continental European countries and Britain.

After some twists and turns, the United Kingdom became a member of the EEC in January 1973. However, after joining the EEC, it showed little interest in issues other than those directly related to its own interests, even though it was one of the major countries in the integrated Europe. When integration reached a milestone and the task of deepening integration became an issue, the British attitude was always reluctant or even negative. This is because they feared that restrictions on national sovereignty would increase. For this reason, Rueff's point of view, even from a long-term perspective including today's, strikes at the essence of the problem.

Chapter 12
Neoliberal Structural Reforms in France

The main positions he held after World War II were as head of the International Reparations Agency, a member of the United Nations Economic and Employment Commission, and as judge of the courts of the three integrated European communities. All positions he held were outside of France, which was undeniably inadequate given his competence and achievements. Postwar France not only inherited many of the organized and centralized institutions from the Vichy regime but also upgraded them through two key policies: nationalization and planning. The majority of the bureaucrats and political leaders were Keynesian, and the parliament was dominated by the left-wing forces of the resistance movement and representatives of the trade unions. It seemed that there was not even a peripheral place for the neoliberal Rueff.

Under the slogan of revival and modernization, France implemented a state-led growth policy, and the economy recorded a high growth rate of over 5% per year on average. On the other hand, budget deficits and overborrowing by the central bank became the norm, and successive governments were plagued by chronic inflation and balance of payments deficits. When these contradictions in postwar policies erupted into currency instability, currency devaluation and austerity policies were implemented. In France, as in the United Kingdom, economic policy was of the stop-and-go variety.

By 1958, however, France's postwar policy had come to a complete standstill. A huge budget deficit and inflation had brought the balance of payments to the brink of crisis, and the country's foreign exchange reserves had nearly run out. The conflict over the independence of the Algerian colony became a quagmire and threatened to escalate into a civil war involving the home country. In continental Europe, the EEC had just been established, but there were doubts as to whether France would be able to implement the provisions of the Treaty of Rome. For the rest of the world, the restoration of currency convertibility was just around the corner. France was in danger of missing out on this trend.

In June of the same year, Charles de Gaulle, the hero of World War II, returned to power as Prime Minister. However, none of the economic experts in and around his government was able to prepare a scheme to deal with the unprecedented economic

Y. Gonjo et al., *The Truth of Liberal Economy*, Springer Studies in the History of Economic Thought, https://doi.org/10.1007/978-981-99-0841-7_12

crisis. At that time, the only one who raised his hand was Rueff, who was a judge of the ECSC Court of Justice. He was allowed to organize the government committee twice under de Gaulle's government and wrote two famous reports in the postwar history of France, "Pinay-Rueff Report" (or "Rueff Plan"), which dealt with financial reform, and "Rueff-Armand Report," which dealt with general economic reform. Rueff also planned to reform the credit system, but a government committee was not established for this reform. The two reports and the credit reform, which was only a private initiative of Rueff, provide a clear picture of the concrete form of neoliberalism in France and, by extension, continental Europe, and the obstacles it faced in the 1960s.

12.1 The Rueff Commission and Fiscal Structural Reform—The French "Miracle"

12.1.1 The Establishment of the Rueff Committee

In June 1958, Rueff met with Antoine Pinay, the Minister of Finance. At the meeting, Rueff explained his diagnosis of the economic crisis in France and how to deal with it, and advised Pinay to set up a committee of experts to draw up an overall plan to overcome the crisis. He then handed Pinay a memorandum that he had prepared, titled "Outline of the Economic and Fiscal Renewal Plan" which contained the following contents (Rueff, 1972, pp. 153–163).

The cause of the balance of payments crisis that France is facing is inflation, and the cause of inflation is the policy of the treasury and the Bank of France. The problem with the treasury's policy is that it repeatedly neglects the budget deficit and takes the easy way out by borrowing from the Bank of France to cover it. The cause of budget deficits lies in the fact that the treasury bears the burden of huge investments, in other words, the "budgeting" of investments. This is because a vicious cycle has emerged: budgeting for investment creates fears of inflation, which in turn stimulates consumption, deprives the market of the few remaining savings, and hinders investment finance. Therefore, inflationary concerns should be eliminated by removing investment from the budget and leaving the financing to the capital market (savings). This was Rueff's proposal for reforming the state finances.

But even more than fiscal policy, Rueff's problem is the central bank's credit policy. Most of the Bank of France's assets (65% of total assets as of May 22, 1958) are in loans to the state and medium-term liquidation notes. Moreover, medium-term liquidation notes recorded the greatest growth throughout the 1950s. Medium-term liquidation bills were bills with a maturity of up to 5 years issued by the nationalized large deposit banks and quasi-public financial institutions such as Crédit National, with the prior approval of the Bank of France, for the purpose of financing equipment, housing construction, and trade. The amount of the medium-term liquidation notes appearing on the balance sheet of the Bank of France indicates the amount of discount on these notes by the bank. In other words, the amount of medium-term liquidation bills was nothing more than the balance of investment finance in "central bank currency." The biggest cause of inflation in France is the discounting of medium-term liquidation notes, which stiffens the assets of the Bank of France. Therefore, it is necessary to ban the discounting of medium-term liquidation notes and leave investment finance to the capital market.

Rueff's memorandum severely embarrassed Pinay. The budgeting of investments and the discounting of medium-term liquidation bills by the Bank of France (the medium-term credit system) were key elements of France's state-led strategy for postwar reconstruction and modernization. Moreover, the central figure who devised the medium-term credit system during the war was Wilfrid Baumgartner, who was president of Crédit National during the wartime, and who was president of the Bank of France after WWII. Pinay withheld his decision for fear that the Bank of France would strongly oppose it. However, the memorandum became known to de Gaulle's bureaucrats, and among them, Rogers Goetze, former head of the price bureau of the Ministry of Finance, showed strong interest in the memorandum. Encouraged by Goetze, Pinay finally agreed to Rueff's proposal.

In September, Pinay sent Rueff back to Paris from his post in Luxembourg and on the 30th of the same month, he set up a special committee, commonly known as the "Rueff Committee" to consider "the general financial problems" of France. However, Pinay's definition of the "general financial problems" referred to the committee did not include credit issues. The Rueff Commission had nine members, including Rueff, all of whom were appointed from outside the economic and financial administration. It worked vigorously and met almost every day from September 30, the day of its inauguration, until December 8.

The members of the committee agreed with Rueff's ideas early on in the meetings, but almost all of the economic and financial bureaucrats who were summoned by the committee disagreed with Rueff's ideas. In Rueff's words, "they had become accustomed to deficits and their financing over the last ten years," and "for them, fiscal technology had essentially become the art of borrowing" (Rueff, 1972, p. 260). Nevertheless, the committee operated under Rueff's leadership from beginning to end and prepared the "Report on the Financial Situation," dated December 8, which was submitted to Pinay (Rueff, 1972, pp. 170–248).

12.1.2 Pinay/Rueff Report (Rueff Plan)

It was Rueff himself who wrote the bulk of the report. As a corroboration of this, the report was anchored on two principles of economic and social intervention formulated by Rueff from 1938 to 1939. The first is the principle that prices and market mechanisms should not be distorted by budgetary subsidies, and the second is the principle that orderly public finance should guarantee the effectiveness of social policies, that is, social policies should be implemented while maintaining fiscal balance and monetary stability. Based on these two principles, the report recommends measures for a fiscal rehabilitation plan, which can be summarized by the following four points.

First, achieve a balanced budget by raising taxes on the one hand and reducing subsidies paid to state-owned enterprises, social insurance, etc. on the other. Second, divest the public treasury of investment finance, which is not backed by financial resources, and leave it to the capital markets. In particular, housing construction finance using the medium-term credit system, which has been a major factor in currency expansion, should be abolished. Third, trade liberalization should be promoted by greatly increasing the number of liberalized items. Fourth, the franc should be devalued. The devaluation of the franc was separated from the main body of the report due to its top secret nature and was conveyed to Prime Minister de Gaulle by secret letter.

The report was firm that implementing its recommendations will end inflation, and capital will flow back from abroad. As a result, the market will be flush with funds, interest rates, especially long-term rates, will fall, and investment will increase. In short, the Rueff Plan was a plan to revive the French economy based on the restoration of the price mechanism.

The draft of the report was written at the beginning of November, and on November 19, Rueff visited the Prime Minister's office and explained the contents to de Gaulle. According to a detailed record Rueff made of this event (Rueff, 1972, p. 251), he explained the contents of the draft report to de Gaulle paragraph by paragraph. Pinay, the Minister of Finance, was also present at the explanation, and he presented an alternative "more moderate and therefore less effective method," which was a partial modification of the recommendation by the Rueff Committee. In other words, to borrow the expression used at the meeting, de Gaulle was presented with two plans, the "strong plan" of Rueff and the "weak plan" of the Minister of Finance. De Gaulle took Rueff's plan and avoided Pinay's plan.

On November 25, Rueff was called to the Prime Minister's Office again and questioned one-on-one by de Gaulle on the Commission's draft recommendations. At the end of this meeting, he and de Gaulle exchanged the following conversation.

> De Gaulle: Your recommendations are excellent in every way. But if I implement all of them without excluding anything [from the recommendations], is this really worthy of shocking the public?
>
> Rueff: I assure you, Your Excellency, that if the entire Rueff Plan is implemented, our balance of payments will be back in balance in a matter of weeks. I have absolute confidence in it. I accept that whatever you think about me in the future will depend entirely on the outcome (Rueff, 1972, p. 251).[1]

De Gaulle asked Rueff for further confirmation on the effectiveness of the plan, and Rueff agreed without reservation.

Apart from theoretical issues, de Gaulle was not the only one who was concerned about the effectiveness of the plan. Even some of the members of the special

[1] De Gaulle asked a similar question to Roger Goetze on December 24. "Exposé de Roger Goetze", in *Charles de Gaulle en son siècle*, t.3, Paris, La Documentation française, p.53.

committee were doubtful. One of the committee members, Claude-Joseph Gignoux, a former president of the French National Association of Manufacturers, frankly confessed his uneasiness in a letter to Rueff. Gignoux first deigns to say that "it goes without saying that the committee's conclusions are impeccable in theory." Then he says, "I wonder if the conditions for the success of the program will not be met. If the subsidies and tax exemptions are abolished, public opinion will react violently, and it is a tremendous illusion to think that the explosion can be controlled by the authority of General de Gaulle." Gignoux concludes: "I understand the argument that you [Rueff] have made again and again, saying that there is no other way but to implement the Commission's proposals, but I think that these recommendations are beyond the bounds of political possibility and that the consequences may be beyond our expectations".[2]

So what made Rueff so "absolutely sure" of his plan? Later in his life, after the "May Crisis" of 1968, he was asked by Maurice Couve de Murville, who had just become Prime Minister, for advice on how to deal with a crisis. Rueff replied to the new prime minister, drawing on the example of his handling of the 1958 crisis, as follows:

To deal with the crisis, we need an "electric shock," and we need a plan. "The plan must be based on the idea that France cannot accept or assume that it will not be able to achieve economic equilibrium, especially fiscal equilibrium, in the long term. To do so, it is necessary to ensure that the budget deficit is brought down below the amount of savings in the market. In 1958, this savings was 600 billion in the old pre-denomination franc—600 billion in the current franc—and the expected deficit in 1959 was 1.2 trillion. As soon as the crisis of money withdrawal and capital outflows subsided, the savings allocated [to cover the deficit] certainly exceeded 600 billion by a large margin, perhaps twice that amount, or 120 billion in today's franc".[3]

In a report he once gave to the International Research Center for Liberal Renewal, Rueff said that fiscal expenditures are effective only if they are made through "deductions from the incomes of individuals through taxes and borrowing," otherwise they are inflationary. It is clear that he regarded this theoretical relationship between fiscal spending and inflation as the core of the problem, and was absolutely confident about it.

Anyway, de Gaulle accepted Rueff's plan and decided to implement it immediately, overcoming the resistance of Pinay, Minister of Finance, and three ministers from the Socialist Party including Guy Mollet, former Prime Minister and General Secretary of the Socialist Party. The Rueff Plan was thus incorporated into the fiscal law for 1959, and the franc was devalued by 17.5%. These measures made it possible to restore the exchangeability of the franc and to open up the French market to EEC members. Inflation came to an end in the first half of 1959. The balance of payments

---

[2] Lettre de C.J.Gignoux à Jacques Rueff, 9 decembre 1958, Cit. par *Charles de Gaulle en son siècle,* t.3, Paris, La Documentation française, p. 167.

[3] Archives nationales, 579AP (fonds Jacuqes Rueff)/161, Note sur la conversation de J.Rueff avec Couve de Murville au sujet du contrôle des changes, 3 août 1968.

improved, and foreign exchange reserves recovered rapidly. Thus, the crisis was literally and "miraculously" overcome (De Gaulle, 1970, p. 146).

The fiscal structural reform plan of 1958 was a great success. For this reason, this plan is widely known internationally as the "Rueff Plan" (that is, of the three plans envisioned by Rueff, this was the highly profiled one.) So what was the key to the success of this plan? In a discussion he had with socialists and trade union leaders in 1939, he made a distinction between "political economy" as a "science" that pursues laws, and "policy" ("policy technology") which is ultimately chosen by the "act of voting" of the people. In accordance with his idea, he succeeded in combining "policy" and "political economy" through the absolute political authority of de Gaulle. It can be said that the key to the success of the plan was exactly here.

12.2 The Rueff/Armand Commission and Economic Structural Reform

12.2.1 The Establishment of the Rueff/Armand Committee

On January 8, 1959, France transitioned from the Fourth Republic to the Fifth Republic. De Gaulle was inaugurated as the first president of the Fifth Republic, and Michel Debré was appointed as prime minister. Despite this change in the political system and the implementation of the Rueff Plan, there was no change in the attitude of the financial authorities toward fiscal policy.

In March, it became clear that Pinay, who remained as Finance Minister, was reluctant to reform. This prompted Rueff to appeal to Prime Minister Debré to continue the reforms. On June 10, he sent a "memorandum on some essential reforms" from Luxembourg to Debré, proposing the following five points: (1) Continuation of fiscal reform, (2) Reform of the international monetary system, (3) Tax reform to achieve fiscal balance, (3) Reform of the tax system to achieve fiscal balance, (4) Reform of credit policy in general, (5) Administrative reform (Rueff, 1959/1972, pp. 265–275).

While preparing the memorandum, Rueff secretly met with Mollet, the General Secretary of the Socialist Party, in Paris. The purpose of the meeting was to obtain the cooperation of the Socialist Party's trade unions in the reform. Mollet had resigned from the cabinet the previous year because of his opposition to the Rueff Plan, but he had changed his opinion of Rueff after the dramatic success of the Plan. At this meeting, he promised to cooperate with Rueff.

However, Debré, who received the memorandum, was cautious and, like Pinay, showed no sign of moving the process. On August 20, Rueff sent a letter to de Gaulle (Rueff, 1959/1972, pp. 275–280). In this letter, he described the situation as follows. Seven months have passed since the adoption of the plan, but there is no movement to advance the reform according to the plan anywhere. On the contrary, "the administration has returned to the world of convention and the passion for reform has cooled. Regulations introduced during the Great Recession of the 1930s remain in place, hindering productivity growth. Subsidies that are no longer needed have not been dealt with." Rueff added that the two national trade union organizations, the General Confederation of Labour (*Force Ouvrière*) and the French Christian Workers' Confederation (CFTC), would also help with the reform. Prior to writing the memorandum, Rueff had met with the leaders of the reformist trade unions through the intermediary of Mollet and had secured their cooperation. Finally, he concludes his memorandum: "Only your personal intervention can put the apparatus [plan] back on track."

De Gaulle responded immediately to Rueff's letter. On September 1, on the instruction of the president, Debré set up a committee directly under the prime minister to study the "obstacles to economic development." In response, Rueff met twice with the aforementioned Mollet, once at the end of September and again at the end of October. The purpose was to seek his advice and cooperation in organizing the new committee. At the meeting, Mollet advised that Prime Minister Debré should be the nominal chairman of the committee and that the two vice-chairmen should be Rueff and Louis Armand, the president of the French National Railways, in order to diminish Rueff's "bad reputation as a liberal economist" (Rueff, 1959/1972, pp.283) and to make it easier to obtain the cooperation of the trade unions. The committee was thus established on November 13, with Debré as chairman, Rueff and Armand as vice-chairmen, and three representatives of employers, three representatives of labor unions, two representatives of state-owned enterprises, two representatives of agriculture, one representative of banks, and three economists as members. The three trade union representatives were to be the General Secretary of the Confederation of General Managers (CGC), the General Secretary of the French Christian Workers' Union, and a representative of the General Confederation of Labour (*Force Ouvrière*). The Rueff-Armand Committee was thus born.

12.2.2 The Rueff/Armand Report—The Idea of a Promethean Society

The committee, which began its work in November 1959, met 95 times before compiling its report in July 1960 (Rueff, 1960/1972, p. 319–448). The report was first prepared by Rueff himself, although his text was moderated because some of the committee members thought the expression was too direct. This chapter will introduce the contents of the report, referring to Rueff's original version.

The report consists of two parts: a lengthy introduction and specific recommendations.

In the introduction (summarized here), the current state of the French economy and the direction of reform are presented in a comprehensive manner. The level of development of the French economy is lower than that of neighboring European countries, the reason being that the structure of the French economy has become rigid due to the various regulations introduced in the interwar period. France should aim for a society that is at the opposite end of the spectrum from the current situation—a society that is constantly being restructured and which is open to scientific knowledge and advances in production technology. The introduction calls this type of society the "Promethean society," after Prometheus, the hero of Greek mythology who stole fire from the heavens and led mankind on a path of adventure. Not only is this type of society the original form of human society, but it is the type that France is forced to choose today, because its final decision to join the EEC will force it to compete on a level playing field with the other countries in the EEC. Let me quote a passage from Rueff's original version.

> For the first time in seventy years, the "liberalization of the exchange rate" [the restoration of the franc's convertibility] has brought the French economy face to face with foreign competition and, above all, with Germany's dynamic production through the Common Market. With the end of inflation and the acceptance of the [European] Common Market, France entered a new era, full of hope but with heavy obligations. With the poisonous support of inflation taken away, the only way for France to develop its own production and improve its standard of living is through effective efforts, constant adaptation to the market, and the pursuit of the highest yields (Rueff, 1960/1972, p. 299).

In order for French society to transform into a "Promethean society" and for economic development to become the norm, rigid factors must be removed from the economy. Once removed, the price mechanism will function normally, the economic structure will be constantly adjusted and reproduced through price fluctuations, and the economy will develop smoothly. This is because "structure and price fluctuations are both the result and the cause of development." Therefore, the "structural reorganization" of the economy must be carried out through the removal of rigid factors by the public authorities. This is the first and core argument of the committee as stated in the introduction.

This argument is complemented by the following two reserved conditions, which can be called the second argument. (1) Since the structural restructuring of the economy will be painful, it is necessary to take "inductive measures" such as interest subsidies, low-interest loans, conversion compensation, housing construction, and education and training. However, in order not to cause inflation, these measures must be kept within the bounds of the "fiscal reconstruction" of 1958. (2) Eliminating rigid factors does not prohibit the public authorities from changing the structure formed through new free price fluctuations in ways such as providing low-rent housing to low-income people. The report states: "We regard price truthfulness as fundamental. But [at the same time] we hope that its effects will be modified, to the extent necessary and possible, by the redistribution of wealth as required by social justice and civilian concerns" (Rueff, 1960/1972, p. 313).

The second half of the report, the recommendations section, identifies specific "obstacles to development" and proposes specific measures. In France, from the Great Recession of the 1930s to the postwar liberation period, the prices of goods and services were successively placed under government control, and most economic activities were subject to a web of regulations. The report examines whether or not such controls and regulations are still meaningful for each individual industry, and suggests specific ways to improve them. The common denominator of these improvement methods is (1) relaxation of controls and regulations (such as the introduction of part-time work) and flexibility of systems and mechanisms and (2) reorganization and improvement of the legal system for this purpose.

What is remarkable in the recommendations section is that three types of reforms are proposed in non-economic areas. The first is "information development," which includes the development of an educational system to train economic experts and thorough public relations by the government on the current state of the economy and economic policies. The second is "education reform," which focuses on developing people's ability to adapt to the marketplace, that is, their ability to "adapt to progress" and "change jobs" based on economic information and government economic policy information. This consists of extending the compulsory education period, introducing basic economic education in secondary education, and expanding educational opportunities for rural residents. The third is "administrative reform," which is mainly aimed at abolishing traditional stove-piped administration.

In short, the proposals in the Rueff/Armand report were nothing more than structural reforms of economic, social and state institutions aimed at increasing the free functioning of the market. Only state-owned enterprises and quasi-public financial institutions, which are deeply political and parliamentary matters, and the credit area, which requires the cooperation of the Bank of France, were excluded from the reform. The full text of the report, with its recommendation of structural reforms based on neoliberal principles, was approved by all members of the committee, including representatives of state-owned enterprises and the three non-communist trade union organizations. It is worth noting that this was in April 1960, when the term "neoliberalism" was still unknown to the general public.

However, unlike the previous Rueff report, the Rueff/Armand report did not immediately lead to the implementation of systematic structural reforms or produce dramatic economic effects, partly because the reforms were too far-reaching. The full realization of the contents of the report would have to wait until the 1980s and beyond, when the trend toward deregulation and privatization of state-owned enterprises took root.

12.3 Credit Structure Reform Initiative

12.3.1 Proposals for Credit Structure Reform

In the two memoranda that led to the formation of the Rueff and Rueff/Armand committees, credit reform was identified as an important issue. However, Rueff was not allowed to take part in credit reform. He wrote in his book that he was "confronted with an absolute ban on credit" (Rueff, 1972, p. 453), which shows how stubborn the resistance of the Bank of France and the Ministry of Finance was to credit reform.

On December 5, 1961, Rueff gave a public lecture on credit reform (Rueff, 1961/1972, p. 469). He begins by outlining the current situation. The inflationary trend in France has not changed since the end of 1958, when the Rueff Plan was implemented. As a result, the strategy adopted in 1958 is about to fail. However, the Bank of France, the party in charge of inflation, continues to repeat the same old argument that the cause of inflation is excess spending by the state. However, inflation since 1958 has been caused by the international monetary situation and the peculiarities of the domestic market, and national finances are not responsible for it.

Next, Rueff analyzes inflation in France as follows. Against the backdrop of a global excess of dollars after the restoration of currency convertibility, a large amount of capital is flowing into France from abroad. However, despite this, there is no adjustment mechanism in place in France to reduce interest rates, especially long-term interest rates, and promote investment. As a result, surplus funds are not absorbed by the market but instead become purchasing power, pushing up prices. So why is the adjustment mechanism not working? There are two reasons.

First, the National Credit Council, which has overall responsibility for credit policy, and the Bank of France, which formulates and implements individual credit policies under it, have set a floor on lending rates for banks (both state-owned and private) which has prevented interest rates from falling (Gonjo, 1999, pp. 267–368).

Second, the "money market" as an interbank market (in the following, the term "money market" will be used in this limited sense) in France is remarkably narrow and almost non-existent. This is due to the French credit system, which originated in the nineteenth century. This system has two major features. The first is that the Bank of France, which has the exclusive right to issue banknotes, sets the discount rate (official rate) below the level of money market interest rates, thereby taking over the liquidation of domestic credit. In other words, the French market is a "central bank market." In addition to general private-sector banks, there is a group of specialized financial institutions called quasi-public financial institutions, which have been established for each economic sector such as real estate, construction, agriculture, and hotels. These financial institutions are created by special laws and are granted privileges such as tax incentives. As a result, an autonomous circuit of funds has formed around each of these financial institutions.

Because of this credit system, France did not have a unified market, as was typical in England. What existed was a collection of narrowly partitioned markets that lacked flexibility. This characteristic of the French market was reinforced by the discounting of medium-term liquidation bills by the Bank of France from the end of the 1930s onward, and became an important factor in inflation. For this reason, in his speech, Rueff severely criticized the Bank of France's credit policy. For example, he said: "The liquidation facilities granted by the Bank of France to holders of medium-term bills are a cancer that has undermined, and continues to undermine, the French currency" (Rueff, 1972, p. 469).

Based on the above analysis, Rueff proposes two reforms. First, the minimum interest rate system introduced during the war should be abolished. Second, the Bank of France will always set the discount rate above the money market rate and will withdraw from the discount business, creating a money market in France. Incidentally, the first means a change in the "organized credit system" since the Vichy era (Gonjo, 1999, pp. 306–336), while the second paves the way for a complete overhaul of the Bank of France's traditional credit policy and the traditional market structure in France (Gonjo, 1999, pp. 1–28). The second reform, in particular, is not an easy task, partly because the Bank of France and the Ministry of Finance have kept the central bank market alive because of the narrowness of the money market.

The Bank of France strongly opposed Rueff's bombshell condemnation of the National Credit Council and the Bank of France, as described above. Baumgartner's successor as governor, Jacques Brunet, met with Rueff on January 10, 1967, one month after the speech. The meeting was attended by the Deputy Vice-President, the Secretary General of the National Credit Council, and the Director General of the National Treasury, the highest officials in charge of monetary, credit, and fiscal affairs in France. However, the meeting did not produce any results, as the arguments of Brunet that the regulatory regime needed to be maintained and those of Rueff that it needed to be abolished ran in parallel and remained unresolved.[4]

In 1962, Rueff was appointed to the Economic and Social Council as a reviewer of the section on finance, credit, and taxation, and he also submitted a memorandum to this state body expressing his views. Thus, from 1963 to 1964, the Council's subcommittee took up Rueff's proposals for credit reform. The Governor of the Bank of France was also invited to this meeting as a witness, and, as in his earlier meeting with Rueff, he made a statement insisting that the regulatory regime needed to be maintained (Gonjo, 2003, pp. 6–7). Thus, Rueff's proposal was not accepted.

As mentioned above, in the area of credit reform, Rueff could not break the stronghold of the Ministry of Finance and the Bank of France, and de Gaulle's intervention was not realized. However, the credit reform was realized gradually and steadily after Rueff left the government. First of all, in the late 1960s and 70s, the bill system was reformed, the Bank of France's market intervention method was changed, and the bank's articles of incorporation were completely revised in 1972. Then, in the 1980s, under the Socialist president François Mitterrand, a large-scale reform of the credit structure, which even de Gaulle had not been able to achieve, was implemented. First, Jacques Delors, the Minister of Finance, enacted the Banking Act of 1984, which mainly abolished the system of specialized financial institutions. Then, from 1985 to 1988, Pierre Bérégovoy, Delors's successor, undertook a major reform of the financial and securities markets, sweeping away the old institutions and practices that had originated in the nineteenth century. In this way, the money market as an interbank market was fully realized in France (Gonjo, 2006, p. 142 et passim). As a result, the Bank of France withdrew from credit allocation altogether and devoted itself to the so-called "maintenance of the stability of the financial system."

The background to the credit reform process since the end of the 1960s has involved the increasing movement of international capital. If the region is limited to

[4] Archives de la Banque de France, Procès-verbaux du Conseil général de la Banque de France, 11 janvier 1962.

Europe, the international movement of capital has been accompanied by the development of the EEC. If the region not limited to Europe, it has been facilitated firstly by the development of the euro currency market and then by the transition to a floating exchange rate system. From the 1980s, a wave of "financial liberalization" spread throughout the world. In order to cope with these major changes in the international market environment, the credit system needed to be made more flexible. Even the leftist government in France had to adapt to this new historical context. To put it another way, political parties and ideological differences no longer matter in the credit sphere (Gonjo, 2013).

Chapter 13
Conclusion

Rueff and Keynes were at opposite ends of the spectrum in theory and policy. Their contrasting positions in the world of economics reflect their different attitudes toward the new political, economic, and social conditions that emerged after World War I. The new conditions shook the very foundations of the Western world, which had previously enjoyed economic liberalism, and threatened to plunge the very modern civilization that the Western world had nurtured into crisis.

Keynes argued that neither politics nor society withstand adjustment through the price mechanism of classical economic theory, but that adjustment was a "fantasy" to begin with, and that the task of his economics was to build a system that did not require adjustment. On the other hand, Rueff believes that if the price mechanism is denied and no adjustment is made at the micro-level, private rights will gradually be restricted, and we will eventually end up with authoritarian regimes and organized economies. He saw the maintenance of a free market economy with a fully functioning price mechanism as a bulwark against the socialism and fascism rapidly emerging in continental Europe.

The Lippmann Symposium in 1938 was attended by French-speaking economists and industrialists, as well as German-Austrian and Spanish liberals who had fled their homelands, but no genuine British-bred economists were present. British economists, not just Keynes, did not seem to feel as keenly threatened by socialism or fascism as the liberals of continental Europe. Their concern seems to have been more with the social and political fissures and fragmentation resulting from the remarkable rise of organized labor. This can be seen in the German transfer debate in the Economic Journal, where Rueff criticized Keynes's thinking for "ending up in the organized economy," to which Keynes did not respond but instead focused on the turmoil that the devaluation of the franc had caused in French society.

The above differences in research attitudes are manifested in the differences in their subsequent theoretical development. In his "General Theory," Keynes started from the "liquidity preference" hypothesis and proposed a policy theory that creates effective demand through monetary and fiscal policies, in other words, a policy theory that requires neither adjustment nor structural change. In contrast, Rueff stays within

Y. Gonjo et al., *The Truth of Liberal Economy*, Springer Studies in the History of Economic Thought, https://doi.org/10.1007/978-981-99-0841-7_13

the framework of the classical theory of economics. Nevertheless, he knew that economics must be able to respond to short-term problems, as Keynes had argued. To meet this problem, he conceived the concept of "liberal intervention" by the time of the Lippmann Symposium (at the very latest). At the same time, he prepared a hypothesis to support the concept that the essence of liberalism is not the realization of maximum utility but the guarantee of a price mechanism. Furthermore, he rejects the traditional understanding of economics as a science of wealth and sees economics rather as "a sort of little outgrowth of the legal system that enforces social peace." Thus, it can be said that both Rueff and Keynes tried to build or reconstruct economics to meet the needs of the new era on the basis of their original hypotheses or original understanding of economics. As for Rueff, he had a vision from early on to create a broad market among Western European countries called the "Common Market" and to realize his own economic and social ideals through this market.

While Rueff and Keynes paved the way for state intervention from very different directions, they both had mechanisms in place to eliminate arbitrariness from intervention. By distinguishing between inflation and "genuine inflation," Keynes limited the meaningful, and therefore permissible, use of effective demand creation policies to underemployment. In his last paper, he also explains the important significance of the "invisible hand" and confirms the limitations of intervention policies. Rueff, on the other hand, limited state intervention to a type compatible with the price mechanism.

In reality, however, it is not easy to put a stop to state intervention. In parliamentary democracies, adjustment through the price mechanism is painful and tends to be postponed by fiscal and monetary policies. Nevertheless, according to Rueff, no society can survive without equilibrium. If adjustments are postponed, imbalances will increase, and the restoration of equilibrium will require larger and therefore more painful adjustments. Even if that is ignored, an uncontrollable economic crisis will eventually ensue, and market violence will force the adjustment. The great recessions of the 1930s and 1970s were the unfortunate consequences of just such postponed adjustments. This is why not only Rueff but also Hayek and other continental European neoliberals did not hide their skepticism about parliamentary democracy.

Ultimately, Rueff was convinced that in a society where individual freedom is guaranteed, the workings of the price mechanism cannot continue to be prevented indefinitely. This view was grounded in his economic theory and his own original philosophy. According to this philosophy, economic theory is formulated by replacing the observable cause–effect relationships in nature with logical cause-effect relationships, and is no different from theories of natural sciences such as physics. Therefore, Rueff does not believe that economic phenomena, which are part of nature, can be freely manipulated to suit human convenience. What humans can do is to develop the technology of economic policy in a way that does not conflict with the laws of nature, just as we can fly an airplane in the presence of gravity. What he calls "liberal intervention" is just such a policy technology.

Rueff analyzed the causes of the French economic crisis of 1958 and the dollar crisis of the 1960s, came up with a way to deal with the crisis, and vigorously lobbied the authorities to adopt it. His determined stance, unconcerned about his isolation at the time, is not unrelated to his philosophical and scientific methodologies as mentioned above. However, it was only in the fiscal structural reform of France under de Gaulle's administration in 1958 that Rueff's recommendations were directly adopted into actual policy. His recommendations were not accepted for the dollar crisis, and the crisis was eventually settled by the collapse of the international monetary system as he had prophesied. This fact is one proof that even if the way to deal with a problem is theoretically correct, it is not always reflected in the actual policy choices. Rueff's tumultuous life as a dynamic theorist and practitioner seems to show us that the history of the twentieth century has been shaped by a dynamism that has its origins in the divergence between theory and reality.

The environment surrounding both Keynesian and Rueffian economics has changed dramatically over time since World War II. First of all, with the end of the war, fascism was swept away from all Western European countries except Spain. At the end of the twentieth century, the Soviet Union, the headquarters of socialism, collapsed. In the 1970s, stagflation caused Keynesianism to expire in most Western industrialized countries, and Milton Friedman's monetarism emerged in the United States as a replacement. On the other hand, Rueff's economics lost its practical basis outside of integrated Europe, as the floating exchange rate system was approved and gold was abolished.

Since the end of the twentieth century, economic globalization has gone hand in hand with financial liberalization, the spread of new information and communication technologies, and the servitization of industries. Many leading companies have made increasing their share of the global market a key part of their corporate strategy. The rules governing the global market are a type of liberalism that could be called market fundamentalism, a freedom without a legal system that resembles "freedom of the jungle." On the other hand, within the nation-state, privatization of state-owned sectors, relaxation of employment and labor regulations, and reduction of corporate taxes are implemented in order to adapt the economy and society to the globalizing economy. In this way, some of the functions of the state are transformed, and the power of trade unions, among other professional organizations, is reduced. Full employment and the welfare state, which had once been spoken of with positive reviews, became dead words. The golden age of the autonomous nation-state and powerful professional associations, which were the premises of both Rueff and Keynesian economics, seems to be a thing of the past.

There is no doubt that globalization has brought about significant changes in the economies and societies of many countries. Nevertheless, the nation-state and the national economies that have spread throughout the world since the nineteenth century are now part of the global world and the global economy. It is inconceivable that they would dissolve. This is because civilized society is ordered by social power, in the style of Rueff. Since there are no international institutions of power in the global world, society must be ordered and maintained by nation-states. Besides, the majority of people spend most of their lives within the nation-state's map. And that's not all. For some time now, the existing international balance of power in the political, economic, and military spheres has been shattered and international tensions have increased. As a result, nation-states are rapidly gaining prominence.

In order for a nation-state to fulfill its expected role, it must have a solid financial foundation. However, after World War I, as the state's intervention in the economic and social spheres deepened, the financial authorities of each country struggled to maintain fiscal discipline. After World War II, Keynesianism was enthusiastically endorsed by fiscal and monetary officials in the West (but not in West Germany, a country with a social market economy) because of the theory's tolerance for budget deficits and inflation. Thus, in the West, a more or less short-sighted optimism took root. According to this theory, even if there is a budget deficit at the starting point, if the economy grows on the basis of a weak currency through aggressive fiscal and monetary policies, the budget will be balanced in the medium term. Rueff severely criticized such optimism and fought against it. He prepared the following theory of growth and concept of social reform as a counterproposal: Growth is achieved as a result of increased productivity at the social level. In order to increase productivity, society must be transformed into a flexible society that is open to scientific knowledge and advances in production technology, and whose structure can be constantly reorganized. In order to remodel society, it is necessary to relax various regulations, implement structural reforms in all aspects of the state structure, including administrative and fiscal reforms, and sweep away the old rigidities, especially the stove-piped administration.

It was not until the 1970s, after the defeat of the fight against severe stagflation, that Western Europeans realized that having a strong national currency and raising productivity was the alpha and omega and embarked on far-reaching structural reforms in line with Rueff's recommendations. In the 1980s, structural reforms and the new economic and social ideals that underpinned them generally reached a national consensus (Gonjo, 2013, pp. 231–85, 543; Gonjo, 2020; Albert, 1982). In this way, the Western European countries were able to quickly align themselves by promoting structural reforms. The reason for this was the urgent need for currency integration in order to protect the European Common Market from exchange rate fluctuations. To achieve this, it was essential to minimize the differences in the basic economic conditions among the countries in the region—"convergence" in EEC/EU terminology—and this is why structural reforms were hastened. Needless to say, the process of structural reform has been full of difficulties and twists. However, even if there was a temporary stagnation, there was no retreat. In this way, Western European countries, once seen as the epitome of old-style societies, have transformed themselves into twenty-first century economic societies.

Because the nation-state is still in existence, both Keynes and Rueff, who were active in the classical era of the nation-state, have not disappeared from the historical stage. Keynesianism has remained as a policy theory that enables growth through fiscal and monetary policies since the 1970s, as countries set growth as a steadfast social goal after World War II. In other words, it has survived as a convenient, short-term policy theory for those in charge of government to avoid social division and guarantee social peace. On the other hand, Rueff's theories, especially neoliberalism, are still alive and well in the EU today. This fact is obscured by the fact that the scope of integration has expanded significantly in tandem with the deepening of integration. There is no doubt, however, that the EU is underpinned by a number of factors, including the following: a single market in which goods, capital, and people can move freely within the region; a single currency area (the eurozone), the ultimate fixed exchange rate system at the heart of the EU, which is both non-existent and virtually "irreversible"; the strict conditions for membership (especially strict fiscal discipline and stable prices) that guarantee the existence of this currency area; a social market economy as a social principle (Gonjo, 2013).

Since Keynes and Rueff, there has not been a theorist of political economy with a conceptual strength comparable with them. However, this does not mean that the problems that fundamentally question the existence of human beings and modern civilization have disappeared. Science and technology will continue to advance, but this alone is unlikely to solve the increasingly serious global environmental problems. Macroeconomic management technology will continue to advance, but it will not eliminate the contradictions inherent in the market economy. It is unlikely that any attractive social goals will emerge that can replace growth and resolve the contradictions of modern society. Apart from authoritarian states, political systems that can replace parliamentary democracy are also unlikely to emerge.

On the other hand, adjustment by the "invisible hand," which Keynes partly acknowledged as important and which Rueff emphasized, is not easy. With the abolition of state-owned enterprises in many countries, the increasing flexibility of employment and labor relations, and the spread of higher education, the "Promethean society" that Rueff once set as the goal of French society seems to have already been realized in many countries. Nevertheless, even within the EU, the free movement of people has caused various conflicts, and the various systems that are supposed to facilitate job changes and migration as a result of adjustment are not functioning as envisioned. At one time, it was said that economic disparities and income disparities among countries and regions would be reduced with the progress of globalization. In reality, however, there are reports from all over the world that these disparities are widening and becoming fixed. The cacophony coming from integrated Europe, the rise of populism, and the conflicts between major powers over trade imbalances are a reflection of this reality.

Thus, there are still many problems in the liberal economy that need to be solved, and the classic debate between Rueff and Keynes, both directly and indirectly, has not faded away even today.

Bibliography

List of archival sources and bibliography.

Archival Sources

Followings are the archival documents consulted in the process of writing this book. Listed below are the institutions, document types, and their contents.

Archives nationales, Fonds Jacques Rueff, correspondences.

Archives Economiques et Financières, Fonds Directeur du Trésor, Reports produced by Rueff as Financial officer staying in London, etc.

Archives de la Banque de France, Fonds de Direction Générale, Procès-verbaux du Conseil Général de la Banque de France, etc.

Hoover Institute Archives, Stanford University, Archives of Friedrich von Hayek, Documents relating to Mont Pèlerin Society (Photocopied documents lent by Mr. Isao Suto).

Selected Bibliography

The printed bibliography below is based mainly on the titles cited in this book.

Albert (Michel), *Un Pari pour l'Europe. Vers le redressement de l'économie européenne dans les années 1980,* Paris, Seuil, 1982.

Bergson (Henri), *L'évolution créatrice,* Paris, Félix Alcan, 1907.

Bourricaud (François) et Salin (Pascal), *Présence de Jacques Rueff,* Paris, Plon, 1989.

Bureau International du Travail, *Dix ans d'organisation internationale du travail,* Genève, B.I.T., 1931.

Chivvis (Christopher S.), *The Monetary Conservative. Jacques Rueff and the Twentieth-Century Free Market Thought,* DeKalb, Northern Illinois University, 2010.

Commissariat Général du Plan, *Jacques Rueff, Leçons pour notre temps (Actes du Colloque pour la commémoration du centenaire de sa naissance),* Paris, Economica, 1997.

Committee on Finance and Industry, *Report: presented to Parliament by the Financial Secretary to the Treasury by command of his Majesty,* June 1931, London, H.M.S.O., 1931.

Y. Gonjo et al., *The Truth of Liberal Economy*, Springer Studies in the History of Economic Thought, https://doi.org/10.1007/978-981-99-0841-7

Compte-rendu des séances du Colloque Walter Lippmann, 26–30 août 1938, Paris, Medicis, 1939.

De Gaulle (Charles), *Discours et messages*, t.IV, Paris, Plon, 1970.

De Gaulle (Charles), *Mémoires d'éspoire. Le Renouveau*, Paris, Plon, 1970.

Gayon (Vincent), «Le keynésianisme international se debat. Sens de l'acceptable et tournant néoliberal à l'OCDE», *Annales, Histoire, Sciences Sociales*, 72(1), 2017.

Gonjo (Yasuo), *Huransu Shihonshugi to Chuuou Ginkou: Huransu Ginkou Kindaika no Rekishi [French Capitalism and the Central Bank: A History of the Modernization of the Banque de France]*, Tokyo, University of Tokyo Press, 1999.

Gonjo (Yasuo), "Huransu ni okeru Shinjiyuushugi to Shinnyou Kaikaku (1961-73)" ["Neoliberalism and the Credit System Reform in France (1961–73)"], *Economia*, vol.54, no.2, January 2003.

Gonjo (Yasuo), ed., *Shinjiyuushugi to Sengo Shihonshugi: Oubei ni okeru Rekisiteki Keiken [Neoliberalism and the Postwar Capitalism: Historical Experiences in Europe and the United States]*, Tokyo, Nihon Keizai Hyouronsha, 2006.

Gonjo (Yasuo), *Tsuukatougou no Rekishiteki Kigen: Shinhonshugi Sekai no Daitenkan to Yoroppa no Sentaku [Historical Origin of the Monetary Union: A Great Transformation of the Capitalist World and the Choice of Europe]*, Tokyo, Nihon Keizai Hyouronsha, 2013.

Gonjo (Yasuo), «Le plan Barre (1976) : origine historique de l'adaptation de l'économie française à l'environnement international moderne», in Danièle Fraboulet et Phillipe Verheyde (dirs.), *Pour une histoire sociale et politique de l'économie. Hommage à Michel Margairaz*, Paris, Editions de la Sorbonne, 2020.

Hartwell (R.M.), *A History of the Mont Pèlerin Society*, Indianapolis, Liberty Fund, 1995.

Hayek (F.A.), *The Road to Serfdom*, London and Chicago, Routledge/University of Chicago Press, 1944.

Institut Charles de Gaulle, *1958. La faillite ou le miracle. Le plan de Gaulle-Rueff (Actes du Colloque tenu par l'Institut Charles de Gaulle le 26 janvier 1985)*, Paris, Economica, 1986.

Institut Charles de Gaulle, *De Gaulle en son siècle*, t.3, Paris, La Documentation française, 1992.

Journal Officiel, *Documents parlementaires, Chambre des députés*, no.3813, 5 juillet 1934.

Keynes (John Maynard), *The Collected Writings of John Maynard Keynes [CWJMK]*, 30 vols., 1981–1989, Cambridge, Cambridge University Press, 1983.

Lippmann (Walter), *The Good Society*, London, Allen & Unwin, 1938.

Minard (Gérard), *Jacques Rueff. Un libéral français*, Paris, Odile Jacob, 2016.

Ministry of Foreign Affairs, *Memorandum on the Organization of a System of Federal European Union*, 1 May 1930, World Digital Library.

Mirowski (Philip), Plehwe (Dieter) (eds.), *The Road from Mont Pèlerin. The Making of the Neoliberal Thought Collective*, Cambridge, Harvard University Press, 2009.

Roosa (Robert V.), *Monetary Reform for the World Economy*, Harper & Row, 1965.

Roosa (Robert V.), *The Dollar and World Liquidity*, New York, Random House, 1967.

Röpke (Wilhelm), *Civitas humana*, Zürich, E. Rentsch, 1944.

Rueff (Jacques), *Des sciences physiques aux sciences morales (Introduction à l'étude de la morale et d'économie politique rationnelle)*, Paris, Alcan, 1922.

Rueff (Jacques), *Théorie des phénomènes monétaires. Statique*, Paris, Payot, 1927.

Rueff (Jacques) et autres, *Les doctrines monétaires à l'épreuve des faits,* Paris, Alcan, 1932.

Rueff (Jacques), *L'ordre social,* 2 vols., Paris, Sirey, 1945.

Rueff (Jacques), «Reply», *Quarterly Journal of Economics,* November 1948.

Rueff (Jacques), *Le lancinant problème des balances de paiements,* Paris, Payot, 1965.

Rueff (Jacques), *Les fondements phylosophiques des systèmes économiques,* Paris, Payot, 1967.

Rueff (Jacques), *Le péché monétaire de l'Occident,* Paris, Plon, 1971.

Rueff (Jacques), *Combat pour l'ordre financier : Mémoires et documents pour servir à l'histoire du dernier demi-siècle,* Paris, Plon, 1972.

Rueff (Jacques), *Oeuvres complètes de Jacques Rueff [OCJR],* 6 vols., Paris, Plon, 1977–1981.

Rueff (Jacques) Vol. I: *De l'aube au crépuscule. Autobiographie de l'auteur,* 1977.

Rueff (Jacques) Vol.II- 1 et 2: *Théorie monétaire,* 1979.

Rueff (Jacques) Vol.III-1 et 2: *Politique économique,* 1979–1980.

Rueff (Jacques) Vol. IV: *L'ordre social,* 1981.

Rueff (Jacques), *Leçons pour notre temps,* Paris, Economica, 1997.

Solomon (Robert), *The International Monetary System, 1945-1981,* New York, Harper & Row, 1982.

Teulon (Frédéric) and Fischer (Bruno), «L'analyse libérale des crises financières : un hommage à Jacques Rueff», *Vie et sciences de l'entreprise*, no. 189, December 2011.

Tobin (James), «The Failure of Lord Keynes' General Theory: Comment», *Quarterly Journal of Economics,* November 1948.

Triffin (Robert), *Gold and the Dollar Crisis,* New Haven, Yale University Press, 1960.

Yago (Kazuhiko), *The Financial History of the Bank for International Settlements*, Routledge, 2013.

Supplement to the Bibliography

Patrick Fridenson

Printed Sources

Roger Goetze, *Entretiens avec Roger Goetze, haut fonctionnaire des finances Rivoli-Alger-Rivoli, 1937–1958*, edited by Nathalie Carré de Malberg, Florence Descamps, Agathe Georges-Picot, Paris, Comité pour l'histoire économique et financière de la France, 1997.

Roger Goetze, *Entretiens avec Roger Goetze, un financier bâtisseur, 1957–1988,* edited by Florence Descamps, Agathe Georges-Picot, and Sabine Effosse, Paris, Comité pour l'histoire économique et financière de la France, 2007.

Bibliography

Bertrand Blancheton, « Jacques Rueff», in Fabien Cardoni, Nathalie Carré de Malberg, Michel Margairaz (eds.), *Dictionnaire historique des inspecteurs des finances: 1801–2009*, Paris, Comité pour l' histoire économique et financière de la France, 2012, pp. 440–441.

Fabien Cardoni, Nathalie Carré de Malberg, Michel Margairaz (eds.), *Dictionnaire historique des inspecteurs des finances: 1801–2009*, Paris, Comité pour l' histoire économique et financière de la France, 2012.

Michel-Pierre Chélini, « Le plan de stabilisation Pinay-Rueff, 1958», *Revue d'histoire moderne et contemporaine*, vol. 48, no. 4, 2001, p. 102–123.

Marie Daou, "Rueff and the liberal social order: an interventionist liberalism", *Journal of the History of Economic Thought*, vol. 41, no. 4, 2019, p. 573–591.

Marie Daou, « L'ingénieur économiste Jacques Rueff: rationalité et expérience. De l'application d'une méthode scientifique aux implications de la statistique en économie politique», *Oeconomia*, vol. 9, no. 4, 2019, p. 627–663.

Y. Gonjo et al., *The Truth of Liberal Economy*, Springer Studies in the History of Economic Thought, https://doi.org/10.1007/978-981-99-0841-7

Marie Daou, « Aux sources conventionnalistes du discours épistémologique de l'ingénieur économiste Jacques Rueff», *Revue de Philosophie Economique*, vol. 22, no. 2, 2021.

Marie Daou « La théorie du chômage de Jacques Rueff. Traitement statistique et méthodologie scientifique», *Cahiers d'économie politique*, n° 80, 2022, p. 35–60.

François Denord, *Néolibéralisme version française. Histoire d'une idéologie politique,* 2nd ed., Marseille, Agone, 2016.

Robert W. Dimand and Harald Hagemann (eds.), *The Elgar Companion to John Maynard Keynes*, Cheltenham, UK, and Northampton, MA, Edward Elgar, 2019.

Barry Eichengreen, *Exorbitant Privilege. The Rise and Fall of the Dollar and the Future of the International Monetary System*, New York, Oxford University Press, 2011.

Olivier Feiertag and Michel Margairaz (eds.), *Les banques centrales et l'État-nation*, Paris, Presses de Sciences Po, 2016.

Julian Jackson, *A Certain Idea of France: The Life of Charles de Gaulle*, Harmondsworth, Penguin Books, 2019.

Matthias Kipping, *La France et les origines de l'Union européenne. Intégration économique et compétitivité internationale*, Paris, Comité pour l' histoire économique et financière de la France, 2002.

Georges Lacan, *Le comité Rueff-Armand et ses retombées immédiates: une tentative prématurée de modernisation (1959–1961)* , PhD in history, Université Paris VIII, 2002.

Frances M. B. Lynch, «De Gaulle's First Veto. The Rueff Plan and the Free Trade Area», *Contemporary European History*, vol. 9, no. 1, 2000, p. 111–135.

Ivo Maes, *Robert Triffin: A Life*, Oxford, Oxford University Press, 2020.

Charles S. Maier, *The Project-State and Its Rivals: A New History of the Twentieth and Twenty-first Centuries*, Cambridge, MA, Harvard University Press, 2023.

Jamie Martin, *The Meddlers: Sovereignty, Empire and the Birth of Global Economic Governance*, Cambridge, MA, Harvard University Press, 2022.

Eric Monnet, *Controlling credit: central banking and the planned economy in postwar France, 1948–1973*, Cambridge, Cambridge University Press, 2018.

Niklas Olsen, *The Sovereign Consumer: A New Intellectual History of Neoliberalism*, Cham, Palgrave Macmillan, 2019.

Elizabeth Popp Berman, *Thinking Like an Economist: How Efficiency Replaced Equality in U.S. Public Policy*, Princeton, Princeton University Press, 2022.

Laure Quennouëlle-Corre, *La direction du Trésor 1947–1967. L'État-banquier et la croissance*, Paris, Comité pour l'histoire économique et financière de la France, 2000.

Laurent Warlouzet, *Governing Europe in a Globalizing World: Neoliberalism and its Alternatives following the 1973 Oil Crisis*, London, Routledge, 2017.

Cecil O. Smith, Jr., «The Longest Run: Public Engineers and Planning in France», *American Historical Review*, vol. 95, no. 3, 1990, pp. 657–692.

Kazuhiko Yago, Yoshio Asai, Masanao Itoh (eds.), *History of the IMF: organization, policy, and market*, Cham, Springer, 2015.

Postface

The new context that the world has been facing in recent years (climate change crisis, energy and food security challenges, the pandemic, war in Europe) gives many observers the feeling that we are entering a new phase of economic history. Simultaneously, it brings to the forefront much older questions: inflation, interest rates, unemployment allowances, currencies, central banks, international institutions, adjustments. All these features give a new relevance to the policies and thoughts of the French high-ranking civil servant and economist Jacques Rueff (1896–1978), one of the leading economists of the twentieth century, a key figure of modern liberalism and a staunch opponent to his older British counterpart John Maynard Keynes (1883–1946), whom he outlived by a third of a century.

Rueff is the core of this new book by Japanese economic historian Yasuo Gonjo (1941–2021), and indeed his last book. This book is a sequel to Gonjo's most recent book, *The historical origins of monetary European integration (1958–1981): policy choices of European countries in the great transformation of capitalism* (2013), a book available in Japanese only. Although he had been using the concept of neoliberalism in publications as early as 2003, it was only when, for the latter book, he read the internal archives of the Bank of France, those of the French president of the Republic and the verbatims of the meetings held by the governors of European central banks in the 1970s that he acquired the conviction that Europe had undergone several structural changes by the mid-1970s. One of them was obviously the conversion from Keynesianism to liberalism of a significant part of the French leading political and administrative elites in charge of macro-economic policies as well as the welfare state. Of course, that finding needed to be explained in the specific European context.

Meanwhile, parallel questions were being raised in the United States. In her 2022 book (Popp Berman, 2022), the American professor of organizational studies Elizabeth Popp Berman has argued that "economic reasoning came to dominate Washington between the 1960s and the 1980s" in terms of framing and debating federal public policy, i.e., the policy of the most important power during that period. She

Y. Gonjo et al., *The Truth of Liberal Economy*, Springer Studies in the History of Economic Thought, https://doi.org/10.1007/978-981-99-0841-7

rather provocatively suggests that "efficiency replaced equality" and that "thinking like an economist" still "continues to constrain progressive ambitions today."

In order to assess this renewal of liberalism and ensuing defeat of Keynesianism, Yasuo Gonjo had in his library a book by French historical sociologist François Denord (Denord, 2007, revised ed. 2016): it showed how in August 1938 a meeting in Paris had gathered 22 economists, sociologists, and philosophers from Europe, two Americans and three French business leaders in order to promote a revival of liberalism, coined at the final stage of publication "neoliberalism". It included major figures such as Austrian economists now teaching in other countries Friedrich Hayek and Ludwig von Mises, the future architects of postwar social market economy in Germany Wilhelm Röpke and Walter Rüstow, and on the French side men like the sociologist Raymond Aron and Jacques Rueff. There the term neoliberalism took off and its fame would expand in the aftermath of World War II. After 2013, Yasuo Gonjo decided to focus on Rueff for two reasons: his doctrinal rigor (at the 1938 Paris colloquium where participants had divided about the goals of the new movement, he had sided with Hayek as a proponent of an unreconstructed liberalism), his almost continuous presence in top bureaucracy on both the French and the international arena.

What accounts for the originality of Rueff when one reads this book?

First, Rueff is typical of a French peculiarity: he is an engineer economist, not an academic economist (as Keynes is). This explains several features of his intellectual and administrative biography. Economics was long underdeveloped in French academia: in universities it belonged to Faculties of law, it maintained a literary character, and law professors kept the control of these Faculties in the interest of their own field. Thus, a good deal of the advancement of economics happened outside academia, mostly among the leading state engineering schools which originate in the eighteen century. This was true of the first state engineering school, the School of Bridges and Highways, established in 1747, as it had to imagine and calculate the costs, traffic, maintenance, and growth of public works. From this initial location, economics for and by engineers expanded to further national engineering schools. It became a matter in the curriculum of the most prestigious of them, the Ecole Polytechnique, founded during the French Revolution, in 1794, which led to the highest positions in government, in the army, and soon also in business. By 1901, economics was no more taught there by economists but by a leading engineer (and alumnus), Clément Colson. An engineer economist teaching engineering students (and doing research): thereafter a second group of engineer economists began to grow, and at the summit of engineering schools. It had three types of consequences. It further contributed to turn the most appreciated type of economics in France into a state knowledge, able to guide governments and policies. As Colson was a thurifer of liberalism, it helped to root liberalism as the doctrine of top civil service. Rueff who was one of the first students of Colson focused on physics to inspire his economic theory in keeping with his engineering education, and he contributed to develop statistics in France to test the feasibility of some of his policies; on the contrary, Keynes, an academic economist, studied mathematics before moving into economics, and he made a major contribution not to the statistical apparatus but to the theory of probabilities (Daou, 2019).

Belonging to the alumni of France's most powerful state engineering school gave Rueff further assets. When he tried to have his liberal views on policies prevail in difficult situations he could rely on the prestige of his school and the support of many of its alumni, also, to some extent, on its and their influence abroad. But this belonging even kept him in the middle of the public space at periods when liberalism was no more fashionable. For instance, during the world depression of the 1930s, three of these engineers created in 1931 a forum to elaborate new forms of state intervention, X-Crise. It attracted initially 12 members, 500 in 1933, 2000 in 1936 (out of whom 500 were not alumni from Polytechnique). For them, it was natural, obvious to hear their colleague Rueff in their meetings, to take his objections into account or to refute them. Hence his famous speech on April 8, 1934: "Why, despite everything, I remain a liberal." Rueff was not the only liberal within X-Crise. His mentor Colson, the economic statistician François Divisia, René Duchemin the head of the French National Association of Manufacturers and Rueff formed the right wing of the forum, the "supporters of liberty", But the center, the upholders of a capitalist economy led by the state, were the majority, whereas the left, the socialists, were another minority (Smith, 1990; Denord, 2016). Conversely, participating to this forum helped Rueff to refine his arguments, and maintaining his position against the current could reinforce his position in government. It also taught him the power of ideas and the role of groups debating outside the framework of public administration to influence decision-making.

Second originality, Rueff, despite occupying a number of international positions during his career (in the League of Nations during the interwar years, and in the new European institutions in the postwar era), did not support global economic governance (Martin, 2022). His own sense of liberalism excluded meddling into other nations' business. This differentiated him not only from the interwar meddlers, mostly British and in minority Americans, but even from a number of French top civil servants or politicians. In that sense, he was the opposite of his much less known contemporary Pierre Quesnay (1895–1937). Pierre Quesnay was a member of the League of Nations Commission in Austria (1920–25), before becoming the Head of the Economic Analysis Department of the Bank of France (1926–29), member of the Young Plan Commission (1929), and an expert for France at the Hague and London Conferences of 1929–30 and the first General Manager of the Bank for International Settlements from the Bank's founding in April 1930 until his death in 1937 (Yago, 2013). In addition, centrist Christian-democrats (Jean Monnet) or some radical socialists (Étienne Clémentel) agreed that global credit markets were incompatible with unlimited democratic sovereignty. Rueff would strive during his entire life to keep the economic sovereignty of the French nation even though he warmly supported European economic integration in the name of wider free markets.

Third originality, Rueff's constant liberalism is shown by this book to be qualified in practice. To be sure, Rueff's criticism of British unemployment allowances of the 1920s and of minimum wages as preventing structural adjustments on the labor market is here depicted in full in the cold and mathematical terms of Rueff's reasoning justified by the target of a return to full employment. Yet, in the mid-1930s, Rueff appears as a "nuanced supporter of deflationary policies" (Chivvis, 2010). The social policy he later favors is supportive of the disadvantaged and is aimed at cushioning the impact of free competition on wage earners (idem). After World War II, when the Mont-Pèlerin Society is founded in 1947 by Friedrich Hayek to promote liberalism and to challenge the prevalence of dirigism and Keynesianism, Rueff soon joins the Society, in 1948. However, he expresses several times his disagreement with most of these liberal economists. He becomes uncomfortable with the idea of spontaneous order now supported by Hayek. Building on his experience at the European Court of Justice, he considers that if the state should not boost demand in the line of Keynes's theories, it is however welcome to intervene by the means of laws and decrees designed to protect market mechanisms against possible abuse. Similarly, European and international institutions should be empowered to limit the voluntarist action of governments in the name of international peace. Thus, Rueff's liberalism proves to be an "interventionist liberalism" (Daou, 2019).

Cogently, the book offers a striking example of the relations between theory and policy as it studies Rueff's influence after general de Gaulle's return to power in 1958 (Goetze, 1997, 2007; Chélini, 2001; Larcan, 2002; Blancheton, 2012). Rueff is fully credited for inspiring and impulsing the triple policy of reduction of the budgetary deficit, desindexation of wages and strong devaluation which led to reduction of inflation, recovery of price competitiveness and a higher pace of growth. However, most of the radical long-term measures and structural reforms that are devised in the Committee that he then chairs together with another leading engineer, Louis Armand, in order to "suppress the obstacles to economic expansion", are not enforced. This contrast needs to be explained after reading this book. On one side, several top bureaucrats, colleagues of Rueff, were not convinced, either by political realism or by adhesion to Keynesianism, and they did not propose these measures to the government. On the other side, the president of the Republic, general de Gaulle (Jackson, 2019), did not support them by his own move. This episode shows a new light on the limits of his presidential power or the hierarchy of his priorities or his sense of political possibilities.

The surprise brought by the book lies in its overall assessment. Relying on his own research about European monetary integration from 1958 to 1981 seen from a French perspective, Yasuo Gonjo assesses very critically the dominance of the United States on postwar world monetary policies and the international balance of payments and the disequilibria and disorders it caused. He shows how Rueff extended the analyses of Belgian economist Robert Triffin against the dangerous increase of monetary bases it fueled (Maes, 2020). Thus, he sides with a number of other historians and economists who have studied the rise and fall of the dollar as "an exorbitant privilege" (Eichengreen, 2011). It leads him further, i.e., to suggest that Rueff's critique of both the abandonment of the gold standard by the US under Roosevelt in 1933 and the postwar limited return in the Bretton Woods international monetary system (Yago et al., 2015) was justified, arguing that a stable and committing mechanism is better than the evils of inflation. Thus Rueff's famous stand of 1965 against the dollar-reserve currency privilege as « feeding the inflationary expansion of credit », hence creating trends « impossible to control » till the break of August 1971 (Maier, 2023), is presented as understandable in many respects. Even more surprising is his subtle criticism of the French state's acceptance of a limited competition between firms before European economic integration and during its early years, as well of the contradictions between the long-term ambitions of French economic planning and the short-term sensitivity of the French state to both home politics and international pressures. It is quite a paradox to see that Yasuo Gonjo, having been trained in Marxist economic history and continuing in the last pages of this book to underline the limits or the negative sides of neoliberalism's influence since the 1980s, still bemoaning "market fundamentalism" and the "widening disparities" of globalization, deeply conscious of the novelty of the current world where the influence of European nation-states is no more the same, comes to support some of the views of a major liberal economist and thinker in what is his final book.

Patrick Fridenson.

The manufacturer's authorised representative in the EU is Springer Nature Customer Service Centre GmbH, Europaplatz 3. 69115 Heidelberg, Germany. If you have any concerns regarding our products, please contact ProductSafety@springernature.com

Printed and bound by CPI Group (UK) Ltd, Croydon, CR0 4YY

30/09/2026

02225260-0019